WORLD WAR I

History SparkNotes

Spark Educational Publishing
A Division of Barnes & Noble Publishing
120 Fifth Avenue
New York, NY 10011
www.sparknotes.com

ISBN 1-4114-0427-0

Please submit all comments and questions or report errors to *www.sparknotes.com/errors.*

Printed and bound in the United States

Contents

Overview

World War I took place between 1914 and 1918. Although the conflict began in Europe, it ultimately involved countries as far away as the United States and Japan. At the time, the English-speaking world knew it as the "Great War"—the term "World War I" was applied decades later. Historians still actively disagree over the fundamental causes of the war. The period leading up to the war was a complex tangle of diplomacy and political maneuvering—many countries debated over strategies and alliances until nearly the last minute—and the first few weeks of the conflict were similarly chaotic and confusing. However, historians agree nearly unanimously about the war's consequences: World War I led almost directly to World War II and set the stage for many other important events in the twentieth century.

By conservative estimates, around 9 million soldiers died in battle—many of them defending entrenched front lines that were so stalemated that they rarely moved even a few yards in either direction. Civilian loss of life totaled an additional 13 million. Epidemics of influenza and other diseases, either induced or exacerbated by the war, raised the death toll by at least an additional 20 million. In total, counting battle casualties, civilian deaths, and victims of disease, the loss of life worldwide surpassed 40 million.

Political tensions ran high in early twentieth-century Europe. Abroad, Europe's great powers were increasingly coming to impasses over the acquisition of new colonies. As the unclaimed lands of the earth ran short, the race to claim them became fiercely competitive. At the same time, the Turkish-ruled Ottoman Empire, which had existed for hundreds of years, was slowly decaying. Greece, Bulgaria, Romania, Serbia, and other southern European nations that had been under Ottoman rule became independent, changing the balance of power in Europe. The many ethnic groups of Austria-Hungary, inspired by these new southern European nations, began to agitate for their own independence. Furthermore, Serbia wanted back the territory of Bosnia-Herzegovina, lost to Austria in a previous war.

At the same time, technological and industrial developments in Europe were advancing with unprecedented speed. Military technology was at the forefront of this trend, and a horrible war using these new weapons was both feared and seen as inevitable. Indeed, World War I turned out to be a showcase of new technologies that would change the nature, speed, and efficiency of warfare in the century to come. Tanks, airplanes, and submarines changed the way wars were fought. Other types of motorized vehicles, such as trucks, cars, and especially trains, vastly improved the speed with which troops and supplies could be deployed and increased the distance over which they could be transported. Guns in all categories, ranging from pistols to major artillery, greatly improved in accuracy and range of fire, enabling armies to fire upon each other across long distances and in some cases without even having to see each other. The machine gun made it possible for a single soldier to effectively take on multiple opponents at once. Chemical warfare was seen on a large scale for the first time, with results so gruesome that most countries vowed never to use such weapons again.

By war's end, the map of Europe began to resemble the one we know today. The German and Austro-Hungarian empires ceased to exist. Much of eastern Europe, in particular, was redivided along ethno-linguistic lines, and Hungary, Poland, Lithuania, Latvia, Estonia, and Finland all became independent countries. Several other nations were awkwardly combined into the countries of Yugoslavia and Czechoslovakia. A major reorganization of the Near and Middle East also took place following the war, establishing the forerunners of the countries we know today as Armenia, Turkey, Syria, Lebanon, Saudi Arabia, and Iraq.

The aftermath of World War I also marked the practical end of monarchy on the continent and of European colonialism throughout the rest of the world. Most European nations began to rely increasingly upon parliamentary systems of government, and socialism gained increasing popularity. The brutality of the conflict and the enormous loss of human life inspired a renewed determination among nations to rely upon diplomacy to resolve conflicts in the future. This resolve directly inspired the birth of the League of Nations.

Summary of Events

The Start of the War

World War I began on July 28, 1914, when **Austria-Hungary** declared war on **Serbia**. This seemingly small conflict between two countries spread rapidly: soon, Germany, Russia, Great Britain, and France were all drawn into the war, largely because they were involved in **treaties** that obligated them to defend certain other nations. Western and eastern **fronts** quickly opened along the borders of Germany and Austria-Hungary.

The Western and Eastern Fronts

The first month of combat consisted of bold attacks and rapid troop movements on both fronts. In the west, Germany attacked first **Belgium** and then **France**. In the east, **Russia** attacked both Germany and Austria-Hungary. In the south, Austria-Hungary attacked Serbia. Following the **Battle of the Marne** (September 5–9, 1914), the western front became entrenched in central France and remained that way for the rest of the war. The fronts in the east also gradually locked into place.

The Ottoman Empire

Late in 1914, the **Ottoman Empire** was brought into the fray as well, after Germany tricked Russia into thinking that Turkey had attacked it. As a result, much of 1915 was dominated by Allied actions against the Ottomans in the Mediterranean. First, Britain and France launched a failed attack on the **Dardanelles**. This campaign was followed by the British invasion of the **Gallipoli Peninsula**. Britain also launched a separate campaign against the Turks in **Mesopotamia**. Although the British had some successes in Mesopotamia, the Gallipoli campaign and the attacks on the Dardanelles resulted in British defeats.

Trench Warfare

The middle part of the war, 1916 and 1917, was dominated by continued **trench warfare** in both the east and the west. Soldiers fought from dug-in positions, striking at each other with **machine guns, heavy artillery**, and **chemical weapons**. Though soldiers died by the millions in brutal conditions, neither side had any substantive success or gained any advantage.

The United States' Entrance and Russia's Exit

Despite the stalemate on both fronts in Europe, two important developments in the war occurred in 1917. In early April, the **United States**, angered by attacks upon its ships in the Atlantic, declared war on Germany. Then, in November, the **Bolshevik Revolution** prompted Russia to pull out of the war.

The End of the War and Armistice

Although both sides launched **renewed offensives** in 1918 in an all-or-nothing effort to win the war, both efforts failed. The fighting between exhausted, demoralized troops continued to plod along until the Germans lost a number of individual battles and very gradually began to fall back. A deadly outbreak of **influenza**, meanwhile, took heavy tolls on soldiers of both sides. Eventually, the governments of both Germany and Austria-Hungary began to lose control as both countries experienced multiple mutinies from within their military structures.

The war ended in the late fall of 1918, after the member countries of the Central Powers signed **armistice agreements** one by one. Germany was the last, signing its armistice on November 11, 1918. As a result of these agreements, Austria-Hungary was broken up into several smaller countries. Germany, under the **Treaty of Versailles**, was severely punished with hefty economic reparations, territorial losses, and strict limits on its rights to develop militarily.

Germany After the War

Many historians, in hindsight, believe that the Allies were excessive in their punishment of Germany and that the harsh Treaty of Versailles actually planted the seeds of World War II, rather than foster peace. The treaty's declaration that Germany was entirely to blame for the war was a blatant untruth that humiliated the German people. Furthermore, the treaty imposed steep **war reparations** payments on Germany, meant to force the country to bear the financial burden of the war. Although Germany ended up paying only a small percentage of the reparations it was supposed to make, it was already stretched financially thin by the war, and the additional economic burden caused enormous resentment. Ultimately, extremist groups, such as the Nazi Party, were able to exploit this humiliation and resentment and take political control of the country in the decades following.

Key People & Terms

People

Prince Max von Baden

The chancellor of Germany during the final months of the war. As Kaiser **Wilhelm II** lost control of the country, Prince Max temporarily assumed leadership and played a major role in arranging the armistice.

Winston Churchill

The first lord of the British admiralty. Although Churchill is better known for his role as Britain's prime minister during World War II, he played a significant role in World War I as well, serving as the head of Britain's navy until he was demoted in 1915 following the British failure at the **Dardanelles**. Shortly thereafter, Churchill resigned his post and went to serve on the western front as a battalion commander.

Constantine I

The king of **Greece** for much of the war. Although Greece remained neutral during his reign, Constantine himself had strongly pro-German sentiments, at the same time that his government favored the Allies. He abdicated on June 12, 1917, under pressure of a threatened Allied invasion. Less than one month later, Greece entered the war on the side of the Allied forces.

Sir Christopher Cradock

A British admiral in command of the Fourth Squadron. Cradock is known primarily for his catastrophic defeat at the **Battle of Coronel** on November 1, 1914, in which he lost his life.

Franz Ferdinand

The archduke of Austria, nephew of Emperor **Franz Joseph**, and heir to the Habsburg throne. Franz Ferdinand's assassination on June 28, 1914, by Serbian militant **Gavrilo Princip**, is widely considered the unofficial start of World War I.

Franz Joseph I

The emperor of Austria-Hungary until his death in late 1916.

Paul von Hindenburg

A German general credited with a major victory over Russia at the **Battle of Tannenberg** in August 1914. One month later, Hindenburg was promoted to commander in chief of the German land armies, the position in which he served until the end of the war.

Erich Ludendorff

A German general who assisted Paul von Hindenburg in achieving victories at the **Battle of Tannenberg** and the **Battle of the Masurian Lakes**. Throughout the rest of the war, Ludendorff continued to serve Hindenburg, first as chief of staff and later as quartermaster general.

Nicholas II

The Russian tsar who committed Russia to the defense of Serbia when Serbia was attacked by Austria. Nicholas II committed to this course only with hesitation and under great pressure from his military advisers. He abdicated in March 1917 after the "February" Revolution and was eventually murdered, along with his wife and children, by the Bolsheviks in July 1918.

John J. Pershing

The American general in command of all U.S. forces in Europe during the war. To the Allies' consternation, Pershing strongly opposed the idea of sending American forces to fight on the front alongside regiments from Britain and France. Nevertheless, he did eventually reach a compromise, allowing limited numbers of U.S. soldiers to do exactly that.

Gavrilo Princip

A teenage Serbian militant who assassinated Austrian Archduke **Franz Ferdinand** on June 28, 1914. Princip was armed and trained by a Serbian terrorist group known as the **Black Hand**. His assassination of Ferdinand is widely considered to be the opening shot of World War I. Princip spent the war in prison, where he died of tuberculosis in 1918.

Maximilian von Prittwitz

The German general in command of the Eighth Army at the opening of the war. In August 1914, in the first battle Prittwitz fought following Russia's initial invasion of Germany, he was defeated, panicked, and retreated. He was promptly replaced by Generals Hindenburg and Ludendorff.

Radomir Putnik

The Serbian chief of general staff, known primarily for leading a successful defense of Serbia during the beginning of the war. In August 1914, Putnik's forces ambushed the Austro-Hungarian army in the **Jadar Valley** and pushed them out of Serbia.

Paul von Rennenkampf

The general in command of the Russian First Army. Following his defeat in the **Battle of the Masurian Lakes** in September 1914, Rennenkampf was dismissed from the army on grounds of incompetence.

Alexander Samsonov

The general in command of the Russian Second Army, which suffered a catastrophic defeat at the **Battle of Tannenberg** on August 29, 1914. Samsonov committed suicide that same day.

Wilhelm Souchon

The admiral in command of the Mediterranean Squadron of the German navy. Souchon led the attack on Russia's Black Sea ports in October 1914, which brought the **Ottoman Empire** into the war.

Maximilian von Spee

The German admiral in command of the famous East Asia Squadron. Spee is famous for his victory in the **Battle of Coronel** against the British admiral **Sir Christopher Cradock** on November 1, 1914. Just over a month later, Spee died in the **Battle of the Falkland Islands**, in which the East Asia Squadron was defeated.

Alfred von Tirpitz

An admiral and first secretary of the German navy. Tirpitz was largely responsible for the buildup of the German navy prior to the war, as well as for the country's aggressive **submarine** strategy. Although the policy was highly effective, it damaged Germany's international reputation, leading to Tirpitz's resignation in 1916.

Sir Charles Townshend

British general in command of the Sixth Indian Division. Townshend is known for leading the British campaign in **Mesopotamia** from 1915 to 1916. On April 29, 1916, he surrendered all 10,000 of his men at Kut, Mesopotamia—the largest military surrender in British history.

Wilhelm II
The German kaiser (emperor) during the war. Wilhelm II was a cousin of **Nicholas II** of Russia and **George V** of Britain; all were grandsons of Queen **Victoria** of England.

Woodrow Wilson
The president of the United States for the entire period of the war. During the first half of the war, Wilson, a Democrat, maintained a strictly neutral position and tried to serve as an active intermediary between the two sides. American neutrality remained a major theme during his 1916 reelection campaign. However, Wilson was soon forced to change his position when Germany began unrestricted **submarine warfare** and the American public was scandalized by the infamous **Zimmermann telegram** in 1917.

Arthur Zimmermann
The German foreign minister responsible for the 1917 **Zimmermann telegram**, which attempted to coerce Mexico into attacking the United States in exchange for financial incentives and a military alliance between Mexico and Germany. The exposure of Zimmermann's communiqué was a major factor provoking the United States into declaring war on Germany.

Terms

Allied Powers
An alliance during World War I that originally consisted of Russia, France, and Britain. Many other countries, including Belgium, Canada, Greece, Italy, Japan, and Romania, joined later as associate powers. Although the United States never joined the Allied Powers—preferring on principle to fight the Central Powers independently—it cooperated closely with the Allied Powers once it joined the war in 1917.

Austria's Ultimatum to Serbia
An ultimatum that Austria issued to Serbia on July 23, 1914, escalating tensions between the two nations. The ultimatum demanded that Serbia crack down on anti-Austrian propaganda in the Serbian press and that Serbia allow Austria to participate directly in judicial proceedings to prosecute the parties guilty of assassinating Archduke Franz Ferdinand.

Battle of the Bight
A battle on August 28, 1914, in which the British Royal Navy baited German warships in **Helgoland Bight** out to sea, where British forces sank three of the German ships with few losses of their own.

Battle of Coronel
A November 1, 1914, engagement in which the German East Asia Squadron defeated a weaker British squadron off the coast of Argentina.

Battle of the Falkland Islands
A battle on December 8, 1914, in which the British decimated the German East Asia Squadron during an attack on the Falkland Islands in the South Atlantic.

Battle of Gallipoli
A lengthy campaign, lasting from April 25, 1915, to January 6, 1916, in which Britain invaded Turkey's Gallipoli Peninsula as part of its effort to force open the **Dardanelles**, the strait between Europe and Asia. The operation failed and cost hundreds of thousands of lives before the British abandoned the operation and evacuated their forces at the start of 1916.

Battle of the Marne
A battle on September 5–9, 1914, in which Allied forces, following their retreat from **Mons**, stopped German forces on the banks of the Marne River and forced them back forty-five miles to the river Aisne.

Battle of the Masurian Lakes
An engagement on September 9–14, 1914, in which two German armies under the command of General **Paul von Hindenburg** defeated Russia's First Army under General **Paul von Rennenkampf**. Russia suffered 125,000 casualties.

Battle of Messines Ridge
An intensive June 7, 1917, assault by the British on German forces in northern France. The British began preparations six months in advance, digging nineteen tunnels under a ridge where the Germans were entrenched and then filling the tunnels with explosives. The operation was a success and forced the Germans to retreat.

Battle of Mons
A battle on August 23, 1914, that was one of the earliest battles on the western front. The German advance in Belgium overwhelmed

British and French forces, who began a fourteen-day retreat to the outskirts of Paris.

Battle of Passchendaele
An engagement lasting from September 20 to October 12, 1917, in which British forces in Belgium continued to push the Germans back. The fighting was especially miserable because it was carried out during a period of heavy rains.

Battle of the Somme
One of the largest battles of the war, fought in northern France from July 1 to November 18, 1916, simultaneously with the **Battle of Verdun**. The Battle of the Somme was the result of an Allied offensive along a twenty-five-mile front. Although it ended up as a small victory for the Allied Powers, it cost them 146,000 lives in order to advance less than six miles.

Battle of Tannenberg
A battle in Prussia (present-day Poland) on August 26–30, 1914, in which two German armies under command of General **Paul von Hindenburg** engaged Russia's Second Army under General **Alexander Samsonov**. It was a catastrophic defeat for Russia, which suffered over 120,000 casualties.

Battle of Verdun
The longest and one of the deadliest battles of the war, lasting from February 21 to December 18, 1916. Germany, hoping to wear France down and inflict large numbers of casualties, assaulted the fortified town of Verdun, which blocked the German forces' path to Paris. The battle ended without a clear victor, despite the deaths of more than 650,000 soldiers.

Black Hand
A terrorist Serbian nationalist group that was responsible for training and arming **Gavrilo Princip** and others who participated in the assassination of Archduke **Franz Ferdinand**.

"Blank Check"
Kaiser **Wilhelm II** of Germany's unconditional promise to defend Austria-Hungary if Russia attacked it while Austria was invading Serbia. The guarantee was made on July 5, 1914, a week after Archduke Ferdinand's assassination.

Casualties
Technically, the term for the total number of people who are killed, wounded, *or* captured in a battle. Use of this word varies, but historians generally follow this convention.

Central Powers
An alliance during World War I that originally consisted of Germany and Austria-Hungary. Other nations, including Bulgaria and the Ottoman Empire, joined later.

Schlieffen Plan
A German military plan, formulated in 1905, that addressed how Germany should handle the threat of a war on two fronts with Russia and France. In short, the plan stipulated that if war were expected, Germany should first attack France before embarking upon military actions against Russia. The rationale for this approach was that Russia would require several weeks in order to mobilize its troops and assemble them along the German border. Under the plan, Germany hoped to overrun France in only six weeks by attacking across France's borders with Belgium and Holland, which were less fortified than the border with Germany.

Triple Alliance
A prewar alliance among Germany, Austria-Hungary, and Italy, formalized in 1882. At the start of World War I, Italy dropped out of this alliance, initially maintaining a neutral position in regard to the war.

Triple Entente
A vaguely defined prewar alliance among Russia, France, and Britain, finalized in 1907. The Triple Entente was not a formal treaty and had little real substance.

War of Attrition
A war in which victory is determined purely by which side is better able to endure numerous, prolonged casualties (as opposed to a war in which victory is determined by accomplishing a specific objective, such as capturing a major city).

Zimmermann Telegram
A January 1917 telegram sent by German foreign minister **Alfred Zimmermann** to the German ambassador to **Mexico**, discussing a secret plan to bait Mexico into attacking the United States. Under the plan, Germany intended to offer Mexico financial

incentives to attack the United States, as well as military support to help Mexico retake its former territories of Texas, New Mexico, and Arizona. British intelligence intercepted the telegram, which was eventually published in the American press, sparking an uproar that shifted American public opinion in favor of entering the war.

Summary & Analysis

The Road to War

Events	
June 28, 1914	Archduke Franz Ferdinand assassinated in Sarajevo
July 5	Austria requests and receives Germany's "blank check," pledging unconditional support if Russia enters the war
July 23	Austria issues ultimatum to Serbia
July 25	Serbia responds to ultimatum; Austrian ambassador to Serbia immediately leaves Belgrade France promises support to Russia in the event of war
July 28	Austria declares war on Serbia
July 30	Russia orders general mobilization of troops
August 1	Germany declares war on Russia France and Germany order general mobilization
August 3	Germany declares war on France
August 4	Britain declares war on Germany

The Archduke's Assassination

On June 28, 1914, the archduke of Austria, **Franz Ferdinand**, and his wife were on an official visit to the city of **Sarajevo** in Bosnia-Herzegovina, a Serb-dominated province of **Austria-Hungary**. During the visit, Serbian militants, seeking independence for the territory, made two separate attempts on the archduke's life. In the first attempt, they threw a bomb at his car shortly after he arrived in town, but the bomb bounced off the car and failed to kill or injure the intended victim.

Later that day, while the archduke was en route to a hospital to visit an officer wounded by the bomb, his driver turned down a side street where **Gavrilo Princip**, a nineteen-year-old militant Bosnian Serb who had been part of the assassination attempt that morning, happened to be standing. Seizing the opportunity, Princip stepped up to the car's window and shot both the archduke and his wife at point-blank range.

Reaction to the Assassination

The archduke's assassination had an incendiary effect throughout Central Europe. Tensions between Austria-Hungary and **Serbia**, which had already been rising for several years over territorial disputes, escalated further. Despite limited evidence, Austria-Hungary blamed the Serbian government for the assassination. Furthermore, it blamed Serbia for seeding unrest among ethnic Serbs in Bosnia-Herzegovina, a province of Austria-Hungary that shared a border with Serbia.

Russia and Serbia

Austro-Hungarian leaders decided that the solution to the Serbian problem was an all-out invasion of the country. However, there was a major obstacle to this plan: **Russia**, which had close ethnic, religious, and political ties to Serbia, was likely to come to its defense during an invasion. Though poorly armed and trained, Russia's army was huge and capable of posing a formidable threat to Austria-Hungary.

Germany's "Blank Check"

Aware of the threat from Russia, Austria-Hungary held off on its attack plans and turned to its well-armed ally to the north, **Germany**. On July 5, 1914, Austria-Hungary sent an envoy to meet personally with the German emperor, Kaiser **Wilhelm II**, to convey Austria's concerns about Russia. The kaiser felt that Russia was unlikely to respond militarily, as its forces were utterly unprepared for war. He also had a close personal relationship with Tsar **Nicholas II** (the two were cousins), so he hoped to smooth things over diplomatically. Nevertheless, the kaiser pledged that if Russian troops did in fact advance on Austria-Hungary, Germany would help fight off the attackers. This guarantee is often referred to as Germany's **"blank check."**

Austria's Ultimatum

On July 23, 1914, the Austro-Hungarian government issued an **ultimatum** to Serbia containing ten demands. The ultimatum insisted that Austria-Hungary be allowed to participate in Serbia's investigation of Archduke Franz Ferdinand's assassination and, in particular, to take direct part in the judicial process against the suspects. The demands also required Serbia to stamp out all forms of anti-Austrian activism and propaganda emanating from the country. The ultimatum, written by members of the Austrian Council of Ministers, was specifically intended to be humiliating and unacceptable to Serbia.

On July 25, however, Serbia accepted Austria-Hungary's demands almost entirely—aside from just a few conditions regarding Austria's participation in the judicial process against the criminals. Austria-Hungary's response was swift: its embassy in Serbia closed within a half hour of receiving Serbia's answer, and three days later, on July 28, Austria **declared war on Serbia**. On July 29, the first Austrian artillery shells fell on Serbia's capital, Belgrade.

The Other Sides Enter the War

After this first military action, a series of events followed in quick succession. With news of Austria's attack on Belgrade, Russia ordered a general mobilization of its troops on July 30, 1914. Germany, interpreting this move as a final decision by Russia to go to war, promptly ordered its own mobilization. Although the Russian tsar and German kaiser were communicating feverishly by telegraph throughout this time, they failed to convince each other that they were only taking precautionary measures. **Britain** made an attempt to intervene diplomatically, but to no avail. On August 1, the German ambassador to Russia handed the Russian foreign minister a declaration of war.

On August 3, Germany, in accordance with the **Schlieffen Plan** (*see* Terms, *p. 11*), declared war on **France** as well. Germany made clear its intention to cross the neutral nation **Belgium** in order to reach France's least fortified border, in violation of its own treaty in respect to neutral countries. Therefore, Britain, which had a defense agreement with Belgium, declared war on Germany the next day, August 4, bringing the number of countries involved up to six. There would soon be more.

Explaining the Start of the War

Some early accounts of World War I treat its start as a chain of almost coincidental events: a mix of unfortunate lapses in judgment on the part of political and military leaders, combined with a tangled web of alliances and defense treaties that triggered declarations of war between countries that really had little reason to be at war with each other. Although these factors were crucial, a number of other important factors were involved.

After all, most of the countries that came to be involved in World War I had enjoyed relatively friendly interrelations right up to the start of the war. For the most part, they shared strong economic interdependencies, and trade between them was brisk, making the prospect of a large-scale war highly unattractive.

Moreover, though several treaties in force at the time did compel certain countries to join the war, it is a mistake to assume that any of them joined the war "automatically." Leaders in each country debated whether to enter the war and generally made their decisions only after evaluating their own concrete interests and risks. Many of these countries had hidden motives and, at the same time, mistakenly assumed that some of the others would stay out of the conflict.

German Motives

Though **Germany** had little interest in Austria's problems with Serbia, it had significant ambitions regarding its other neighbors. In recent years, Russia had become increasingly involved in European affairs, while simultaneously modernizing and expanding its military. German military leaders felt that war with Russia was inevitable at some point. Therefore, they argued, it would be far better to fight Russia now, while its army was still poorly armed and untrained, rather than to wait until it could pose a greater threat. Some historians claim that Germany deliberately encouraged Austria to go to war with Serbia in order to set off a war with Russia.

Furthermore, German military leaders believed there was a good chance that Britain would remain neutral and that France also might stay at arm's length, despite its treaty with Russia. This wishful thinking helped the German military leaders convince themselves that the war would be winnable and also helped them to sell their plan to the kaiser.

British Motives

For centuries, **Britain** had been the greatest naval power in the world and also had the largest collection of colonies. In the first years of the twentieth century, however, Germany made a massive and costly effort to build up a comparable naval fleet of its own, with the specific goal of matching Britain on the high seas. Germany also had recently shown a stronger interest than before in acquiring new colonies. Britain, seeing these developments as a dangerous threat to the balance of power in Europe, argued to Germany (through diplomatic channels) that the country had no need for a large navy or a large number of colonies. Germany ignored Britain's rebuffs and continued as before. Just as some German leaders favored an "anticipatory" war against Russia, some British leaders felt similarly about Germany.

French Motives

In 1871, **France** had lost the territories of **Alsace** and **Lorraine** to Germany in a war—a bitterly humiliating blow that left France desperate to regain these lands. While fearful of an all-out German invasion, some French leaders felt that if Germany were distracted by a war with Russia, France might have a chance to seize Alsace and Lorraine.

Russian Motives

Russia's motives for entering the war are less clear-cut. The period just prior to the war was a time of great instability in Russia: never before in the nation's history had the tsar's grip on power been so fragile. On the other hand, there was support in Russia for the Serbian cause, and a military victory would likely help the tsar politically. Nevertheless, war was a risky proposition given the poor state of the Russian military at the time. Tsar Nicholas II, who was personally hesitant about joining the war, briefly flip-flopped over ordering mobilization. Ultimately, however, he caved under pressure from overly optimistic Russian military leaders and advisers who had strong nationalistic leanings.

Opening Moves

Events	
August 3, 1914	German troops enter Belgium
August 4	German troops enter Poland (Russian territory) and take three towns
August 5	Germans encounter first serious fighting at Liege, Belgium
August 10	France declares war on Austria-Hungary
August 12	First British troops cross English Channel into France Britain declares war on Austria-Hungary Austrian troops enter Serbia at Sabac
August 15	Liege falls
August 17	Russian troops enter East Prussia (Germany)
August 18	Russian troops enter Austria-Hungary
August 20	Germans enter Brussels, completing occupation of Belgium
August 23	Japan declares war on Germany
August 26	Battle of Tannenberg begins on eastern front
August 30	Russian forces under Samsonov defeated at Tannenberg
September 9	Battle of the Masurian Lakes begins
September 14	Russian forces retreat after defeat at Masurian Lakes

Key People	
Radomir Putnik	Serbian general who ambushed Austro-Hungarian forces in the Jadar Valley
Alexander Samsonov	Russian general who committed suicide after disastrous loss at Tannenberg
Paul von Hindenburg	More experienced German general who replaced Prittwitz and routed Russians at Tannenberg and the Masurian Lakes
Maximilian von Prittwitz	German general who ordered a hasty retreat from Russian forces but was replaced by Hindenburg before his plan could be implemented
Paul von Rennenkampf	Russian general who sustained massive casualties retreating from the Masurian Lakes

Germany's Attack on Belgium

After the initial round of war declarations, events unfolded quickly as each side tried to position itself advantageously. **Germany**'s troops were the first to move, and their initial target was **Belgium**. The first German troops crossed the border on the night of August 3, 1914, expecting to overtake the little nation quickly and to move on to their main objective of **France**.

The Germans found more resistance than anticipated, however, especially among **civilian snipers** who fired on them from hidden positions. In retaliation, the Germans burned a number of towns and villages to the ground and executed large numbers of civilians,

SUMMARY & ANALYSIS

including women and children. The heaviest fighting was around the fortress at **Liege**; the capital, **Brussels**, did not fall until August 20. All the time, however, additional German armies were gathering along the remainder of France's eastern borders.

Russia's Attack on Germany

Undermining Germany's **Schlieffen Plan**, **Russian** troops attacked Germany much sooner than expected. Two Russian armies, under generals **Alexander Samsonov** and **Paul von Rennenkampf**, crossed Germany's border in **East Prussia** on August 17. With the brunt of German forces focused on France, the Russians advanced quickly at first and soon threatened the regional capital of **Königsberg** (present-day Kaliningrad).

Vastly outnumbered and initially overwhelmed, the German commander in the region, General **Maximilian von Prittwitz**, panicked and tried to call a retreat, against the advice of his staff. To deal with the emergency, German military leaders quickly replaced Prittwitz with a more experienced leader, General **Paul von Hindenburg**, and recalled some of the troops from the western front to help in the east.

The Battle of Tannenberg

Reinforced and under new leadership, the German forces in the east struck back decisively at the invading Russian forces. Because the armies of Samsonov and Rennenkampf were operating separately, without mutual coordination, the Germans were able to deal with them one at a time. Two German armies engaged Samsonov's forces at **Tannenberg** on August 26. Eventually, weakened by constant pounding from German artillery, Samsonov's troops were forced to retreat. As they did so, a second German army cut off their path, completely entrapping them. A slaughter ensued in which over 30,000 Russian soldiers were killed and an additional 92,000 taken prisoner. General Samsonov committed suicide that same day.

The Battle of the Masurian Lakes

On September 9, Hindenburg's troops took on Rennenkampf's army at the nearby **Masurian Lakes**, for a near repeat performance of Tannenberg. Though Rennenkampf's army did manage to retreat successfully, they did so only with another 125,000 casualties. Between Tannenberg and the Masurian Lakes, Russia lost approximately 300,000 soldiers in less than a month of fighting.

Austria-Hungary's Losses

While Russia was suffering huge loses against Germany, it did win a victory against **Austria-Hungary**. On August 18, a third Russian army entered **Galicia**, a region along Austria-Hungary's eastern border. The general of the Austrian forces misjudged where the main Russian attack would fall, so the armies passed each other and ended up literally chasing each other around in a circle. As a result, the Russian army was able to push deep into enemy territory and force the Austro-Hungarian forces to retreat one hundred miles with massive casualties.

In the meantime, Austria-Hungary was also losing its first major battle against **Serbia**. On August 12, Austria launched a ground invasion into Serbia at the town of **Sabac**. Though the town was quickly captured, the Austrian army soon ran into a brick wall as Serbian forces under General **Radomir Putnik** advanced up the **Jadar Valley**, ambushing the Austro-Hungarian forces. After a battle of several days, the Serbian armies forced the Austrians to retreat all the way back to the border.

Japan's Entry into the War

On August 23, 1914, **Japan** declared war on Germany in solidarity with Britain. One reason for this action was Japan's intent to retake some islands in the Pacific Ocean that Germany had seized as colonies in recent decades.

Assessing the First Month of the War

The bold, risky steps that Germany and Russia took in the war's opening month had a profound effect on the dynamics of the rest of the war and provided early hints that the war might last much longer than expected. Even in the first days of the war, Germany's much-touted Schlieffen Plan began to unravel, as Russian troops arrived at the German borders faster than anticipated. Although Germany successfully thwarted the Russians, it was forced to divert armies from its advance to the west. Meanwhile, the stiff resistance from Belgium during that western advance indicated that the conquest of France might likewise be more difficult than expected. On the other side, the massive losses that Russia suffered in the first month offered a similar warning sign of how costly and difficult the war might turn out to be.

Germany's Assault on France

Events	
August 23, 1914	Battle of Mons; British and French troops begin 120-mile retreat
September 4	Allied retreat halted at the river Marne
September 5	Battle of the Marne begins
September 9	Germans begin forty-five-mile retreat back to the river Aisne

The Battle of Mons

After completing their occupation of **Belgium** on August 20, 1914, German forces moved quickly upon **France** with two armies. Although fighting between French and German forces had taken place in the region of **Alsace-Lorraine** in southeastern France, the first joint French-British encounters with Germany occurred near the town of **Mons** along the Franco-Belgian border on August 23, 1914.

As French and British armies tried to halt the advancing Germans, they found themselves under heavy fire from long-range German artillery. With the German troops still well outside the range of their own guns, the Allied Powers were quickly forced to retreat. The allied retreat continued for two full weeks, allowing the Germans to advance over 120 miles to the river **Marne**, on the outskirts of **Paris**. For the Germans, the advance was not an easy one. As they retreated, the French and British armies took every opportunity to fight back and to hold each piece of ground for as long as they could.

The Battle of the Marne

On September 4, the Allied retreat was halted. The exhausted and sleep-deprived German troops faced an Allied defense reinforced with fresh troops brought in from Paris. On September 5, a decisive battle began that lasted five days. More than a million troops fought on each side as the Allies made their stand, determined to prevent the fall of Paris.

As the Germans drove at Paris from the southeast, a gap emerged between the German First and Second armies, and British and French commanders seized the opportunity to split the German forces apart by moving into the gap. French reservists were even ferried in to fill the breach using streams of taxicabs. The Germans were never able to regroup.

Formation of the Western Front

On September 9, after four days of intense fighting, the German armies found themselves unable to maintain their position on the

Marne and began to fall back. British and French forces pursued the Germans doggedly and were able to drive them back forty-five miles, all the way back to the river **Aisne**. At this point, the Germans managed to dig in successfully and hold their position, taking advantage of a shorter **supply line**. A deadlock ensued, with neither side able to budge the other. The **western front** that formed would remain centered near this position for the rest of the war.

Failure of the Schlieffen Plan

The aborted German invasion of France, though just a month into the war, marked a major turning point. Although World War I continued for four more years, this first failed advance is often cited as the point when Germany lost the war it had entered with such confidence. Unable to conquer France outright, Germany became mired in a war on multiple fronts. The **Schlieffen Plan**, according to which Germany would have quickly attacked and defeated France before Russia could mobilize and attack Germany, had failed. German military leaders, failing to adapt their strategy to cope with the new situation, suddenly faced a long, drawn-out war on an entrenched front.

Reasons for Germany's Failure

The German invasion of France failed for several reasons, although historians disagree about which was the most important. First, the **unexpectedly early Russian attack** in the east forced Germany to divert some of its troops from the west in order to help fight the Russians.

Second, the Germans did not foresee **Britain's entry into the war** and did not alter their plans when Britain did so. The British Expeditionary Force in France reinforced the French armies and gave them an edge, especially since Germany was fighting with fewer troops than originally planned.

Third, Germany overextended itself by **advancing too far** with the limited forces it had at its disposal. The farther into France the Germans pushed, the longer their supply line became. Ultimately, troop rotation became impossible—a crucial factor considering that by the end of the Battle of the Marne, the German armies had been marching on foot for more than a month with little if any sleep.

Finally, the **diversion of the German First Army** to the southeast split Germany's forces in two, thus increasing their vulnerability to attack. The Allies were able to exploit this division and force Germany backward, stopping German momentum and miring the war in an entrenched front.

The War at Sea

Events	
August 28, 1914	Battle of the Bight
September–October	Several British cruisers are sunk by German U-boats
October 29–30	*Goeben* and *Breslau* attack Russian ports on Black Sea
November 1	Battle of Coronel Russia declares war on Ottoman Empire
November 4–5	France and Britain declare war on Ottoman Empire
December 8	Battle of the Falkland Islands

Key People	
Sir Christopher Cradock	British admiral defeated by Spee's forces at the Battle of Coronel
Wilhelm Souchon	German admiral whose joint operations with Turkey embroiled that nation in the war
Maximilian von Spee	Commander of the German East Asia Squadron; won at Coronel but was defeated at the Falkland Islands

The Battle of the Bight

The war on land quickly spread to the sea, with the first major battle on the water occurring on August 28, 1914, in a corner of the North Sea known as **Helgoland Bight**. The bight, a partly enclosed patch of water on the north coast of Germany, sheltered several German naval bases and offered a good position from which Germany could strike out at Britain. However, the cautious German High Seas Fleet rarely sailed far from port.

Eager for a fight, two British commodores, **Reginald Tyrwhitt** and **Roger Keyes**, conceived a plan to bait the Germans into the open sea, where they would be vulnerable. Under the plan, a small group of British ships would venture into the bight until spotted by German patrols and would then turn and flee out to sea, where a larger British force would be waiting.

In spite of some minor mishaps, the plan succeeded. For the first couple of hours, German ships slipped in and out of a thick fog bank to fire on the British ships. In time, however, the Germans were lured into open water. After a battle that lasted nearly eight hours, Germany lost three cruisers and 1,200 men, while Britain lost only thirty-five sailors and not a single ship. This early defeat intimidated Kaiser **Wilhelm II**, who insisted that the German navy, of which he was very proud, be kept off the open seas and used primarily as a defensive weapon.

Early German Submarine Exploits

The German **submarine** fleet, however, was used aggressively. Submarines armed with **torpedoes** were a new type of weapon at the time, and while many military leaders viewed them with skepticism and even disdain, they proved quite effective. Although the Germans had been developing a fleet of large warships in recent years, they recognized that it was still far inferior to that of Britain. It was almost by accident that they realized the edge that their experimental fleet of submarines gave them.

During September and October 1914, German **U-boats** sank four British armored cruisers and warships, killing more than 2,000 sailors. British naval commanders quickly became wary of this threat and therefore kept their fleet well clear of the waters of the North Sea. Though Britain did have a submarine fleet of its own, British naval leaders generally considered submarines to be "cowardly weapons" and discouraged their use.

Mining the North Sea

Another "cowardly weapon" played a major role in the war at sea—**mines**. Under a treaty signed at the Hague in 1907, sea mining was limited to areas within three miles of an enemy's coastline, so as not to endanger neutral ships. However, both Britain and Germany quickly came to ignore this agreement, and the North Sea became a place of great danger to all ships that dared enter it. This situation was especially problematic for the neutral countries of Norway and Sweden, which depended heavily on the North Sea for commerce.

Turkey and the War at Sea

The war at sea soon brought the **Ottoman Empire**, previously an officially neutral power, into the fray. At the start of the war, the Ottoman Empire, centered on what is now **Turkey**, had remained neutral but generally was friendlier with the Central Powers than with Britain, France, and Russia. Germany was anxious for more allies, especially in the Mediterranean, and high-placed Ottoman officials—such as Minister of War **Enver Pasha**—believed that an alliance with Germany could help bolster the faltering empire, then known as the "sick man of Europe." In a secret treaty signed on August 2, 1914, Turkey promised to aid Germany in the event that Russia attacked Austria-Hungary.

Later that month, two German warships, the ***Goeben*** and the ***Breslau***, docked in Constantinople, avoiding pursuit by the British navy. The Ottomans bought the ships and renamed them, incorporating them into the Ottoman navy. The sale was primarily technical, as German crews would be allowed to remain on board and in control of both vessels.

On October 27, the *Goeben* and the *Breslau*, now sailing under Ottoman flags, entered the Black Sea, ostensibly to practice maneuvers. On October 29, under the command of German Admiral **Wilhelm Souchon** (who may have been working in collaboration with Turkish Minister of War, Pasha), the two ships appeared unexpectedly off the Russian coast, fired on several Russian seaports, sank a Russian gunboat and six merchant ships, and set fire to a Russian oil depot. Russia, believing that the attack had come from Turkey, promptly began an invasion of Turkey from the east. Britain and France also responded by attacking Turkish forts along the Dardanelles. Turkey then responded by declaring war on all three. In a single stroke, Admiral Souchon had helped manipulate the Turks into entering the war on the German side.

THE BATTLE OF CORONEL

Not long after Turkey became involved, the sea war spread even further, to **South America**. The German East Asia Squadron, a small defensive fleet under Vice Admiral **Maximilian von Spee**, had been based on the Caroline Islands in the western Pacific, near China, when the war broke out in August 1914. However, Spee knew that his ships would never be able to stand up against the Japanese navy, which would soon move against him (Japan had entered the war on August 22). Therefore, the East Asia Squadron fled the area and set forth on a two-month journey across the Pacific Ocean to **Chile**, which had a large German population and would offer a safer base of operations from which Spee could prey upon British shipping routes.

On November 1, the German East Asia Squadron encountered the British West Indian Squadron, which had been diverted from its patrol duties in South America and the Caribbean specifically to destroy Spee's forces and remove the threat to British shipping routes. The British squadron, led by Rear Admiral **Sir Christopher Cradock**, consisted of obsolete cruisers ill-matched for a fight with Spee's faster and better-armed ships. In the **Battle of Coronel** that ensued, Cradock's squadron was obliterated, and two ships were lost. Cradock himself perished, along with 1,600 British sailors—the Royal Navy's first defeat in a hundred years.

The Battle of the Falkland Islands

A month later, on December 8, 1914, the Royal Navy had an opportunity to take revenge on Admiral Spee, whose East Asia Squadron had by this time made its way around Cape Horn and into the South Atlantic. Spee's task was merely to disrupt British trade and supply routes as much as possible, but he also made a fateful decision to attack the British colony on the **Falkland Islands** off of Argentina, which he believed would be undefended and an easy victory. Spee's aims in this attack were to destroy the British coaling station and radio station there, which was critical to British military communications. The mission was a fatal mistake.

As it turned out, an entire British squadron happened to be in port that morning taking on coal. The squadron was far better equipped than Cradock's had been, with two modern battle cruisers that were faster and better armed than Spee's ships. The all-day pursuit and battle that followed resulted in the destruction of the German East Asia Squadron: Spee went down with his ship, the *Scharnhorst*, and three other German ships and 2,100 German sailors were also lost.

Importance of the War at Sea

The range and power of the warring nations' naval fleets, along with their ambition to control the world's waterways, were major reasons that World War I spread so quickly. Naval warfare had always been unpredictable (because of the role of weather and other factors), but new technologies made it even more so. Mines, torpedoes, and submarines introduced new threats that made even the greatest warships vulnerable. Compared to giant dreadnoughts, which took years to build and were manned by hundreds of men, submarines were cheap and generally used a crew of fewer than two dozen. Mines were cheaper still and, once laid, required no crew at all.

However, both Britain and Germany were still deciding how best to use these new naval forces, and both were reluctant to commit their main fleets to heavy battles. The Battle of Coronel, the Battle of the Falkland Islands, and other early sea battles quickly made it clear how naval warfare could be used to project power over long distances. In World War I, naval power was more often used to maintain control of trade routes than to capture new territory. As it turned out, great sea battles between large surface fleets were rare in the war; instead, the submarine came to own the seas, and Germany became the undisputed master at employing this new technology.

The War in the Air

Birth of a New Weapon

In the summer of 1914, the **airplane** was less than eleven years old. Aviation was a fledgling technology that fascinated many but still generated skepticism when it came to practical applications. Most airplanes of the time were slow, flimsy contraptions with barely enough power to lift a single pilot and perhaps one passenger. While numerous countries had shown an interest in military aviation, the concept of using airplanes to wage war was still a fairly radical idea. All that changed during the course of World War I.

Reconnaissance Planes

Early in the war, military strategists realized that aircraft could be very useful for **spying** on enemy troop movements. Thus, the **reconnaissance plane** was born—a tool that all sides in the war used to varying degrees. These aircraft typically carried a pilot and an observer with a camera, who would photograph troop positions on the ground. The use of aircraft for reconnaissance grew rapidly during the first few months of the war and played an increasingly crucial role in achieving victories. Such aircraft proved vital to the British and French forces during the **Battle of Mons** and the **Battle of the Marne**, for example.

Fighter Planes

As aerial reconnaissance became more common, so did the need for ways to *stop* enemy observation planes. One way was by firing upon them from the ground, which was ineffective until guns could be better adapted for the purpose. The other way was to develop a means for one aircraft to attack another. The first such attempts were made using the observation aircraft themselves, as pilots and observers attempted to shoot at other planes using rifles and even pistols—a method that quickly proved hopeless. Some pilots tried throwing hand grenades, bricks, or even long ropes with grappling hooks at planes below them. The ideal solution was the **machine gun**, which could fire a continuous stream of bullets, significantly increasing the chance of hitting a target.

Machine guns tended to be large and heavy, however, and only a few were small and light enough to be practicable for use on an airplane. Another problem was that firing sideways seriously decreased accuracy, while firing forward meant that the airplane's propeller would be in the way. The problem was not solved until mid-1915, when a Dutch aircraft designer named **Anton Fokker** developed the "interrupter gear," a timing mechanism that synchronized the machine gun with the moving propeller blades.

On August 1, 1915, German pilots **Oswald Boelcke** and **Max Immelmann** became the first pilots to shoot down another aircraft using Fokker's new method. This development gave the Germans a strong advantage for several months until French and British designers succeeded in adapting the device for their own use about one year later.

Bombers

Bombing was an obvious offensive tactic for use in air warfare, but different countries approached the concept in different ways. Russia was the first to develop an airplane specifically for this purpose: the Murometz, a large four-engine airplane that **Igor Sikorsky** had developed in 1913 as a passenger plane, was adapted for use as a bomber in 1914 and was used successfully throughout the war.

Zeppelins

Germany took a different approach to bombing by using lighter-than-air **dirigibles**, or **zeppelins**, to drop bombs on targets as far away as London and Paris. The slow-moving zeppelins, which had a long range and could carry a relatively large cargo of explosives, reached the peak of their success early in the war, during 1915. As the war continued, the giant airships became increasingly vulnerable to the rapidly improving capabilities of fighter planes: the zeppelins were filled with hydrogen, so only a small spark was necessary to cause the entire ship to explode in flames. As a result, Germany turned more and more to using airplanes as bombers.

Myths and Realities of Air Warfare

As the war went on and airplane technology improved, large battles in the sky became an ever more common occurrence, and fantastic legends and stories grew around great air aces, such as Manfred von Richthofen (the **"Red Baron"**) and Eddie Rickenbacker. These men came to be seen by the public as modern-day knights, fighting a more exotic and elegant war than the grotesque nightmare happening on the ground below.

The truth was quite different. Newly recruited pilots were often sent into the skies with only a crude understanding of how to fly (typically less than five hours training). As the war progressed, it actually became unusual for a new pilot to survive the first few weeks of his duty. Due to this lack of experience, pilots not only fell victim to enemy aces but also succumbed regularly to bad weather, mechanical problems, or loss of control due to pilot error. It was also common for pilots simply to become lost and then run out of fuel over enemy lines. Most of those who were shot down lost their lives not in spectacular dogfights but after being shot from behind without ever having even been aware of their attackers. Although parachutes had been invented decades before, pilots from some countries—Britain in particular—were not allowed to carry them, because military leaders believed their use to be cowardly.

Overall Importance of the Air War

On the whole, aerial warfare cannot be said to have played a fundamental role in World War I, as it did in World War II. Bombing served more as a psychological weapon than a practical one, and the technology necessary to cause the kind of massive damage that bombing would be able to inflict in the near future had not yet been developed.

On the other hand, World War I itself encouraged the rapid improvement of the airplane, both in general and specifically as a weapon. During the four years of conflict, the overall stability and safety of flying improved tremendously, as did the power, speed, and maneuverability of the newest designs. Moreover, the war fostered the general public's respect for aviation and spawned a new generation of pilots and aircraft designers, who would go on to take human flight to the next level after the war.

The War in the Near East

Events

November 5, 1914	British forces launch attack on Basra, Mesopotamia
March 18, 1915	Britain and France attack the Dardanelles
May–June	British forces in Mesopotamia advance up the Tigris
June 27	British forces begin attack on Nasariya
April 25	Invasion of Gallipoli begins
September 28	British forces occupy Kut
November 22	British forces attack Ctesiphon
November 25	British forces retreat after major defeat at Ctesiphon
December 10	British begin evacuation of Gallipoli
January 9, 1916	Last British troops leave Gallipoli
April 29	British forces surrender to Turks after being driven back to Kut

Key People

Winston Churchill	First lord of the British Admiralty; demoted and eventually resigned after British invasion of Turkey became a quagmire
Charles Townshend	Military commander who led British forces in Mesopotamia; forced to surrender at Kut in April 1916

The Importance of the Dardanelles

If any single piece of real estate was believed to hold the key to winning the war, it was the lands surrounding the **Dardanelles**, the narrow strait separating Europe from Asia in northwestern Turkey. Control of the only waterway between the **Black Sea** and the **Mediterranean Sea** was crucial both economically and militarily. Turkey's entrance into the war in November 1914 placed the Dardanelles squarely in German hands, physically separating the Russian and Allied naval forces and effectively preventing them from cooperating. German control of the strait also meant that Russian wheat could not be shipped to Britain and that British military equipment could be shipped only by means of a treacherous northern route to the Russian ports of Murmansk and Arkhangelsk.

Britain's Plans for the Dardanelles

From the time that Turkey entered the war in November 1914, **Winston Churchill**, first lord of the British Admiralty, began working on a plan to reopen the Dardanelles. The British military leadership believed that this goal could be achieved without ground forces, using naval power alone. Given the significant losses the British army suffered defending France against the Germans, this idea of a navy-only campaign for the Dardanelles was politically important. On November 3, two days after Turkey entered the war, British and French ships made a brief military demonstration by firing on the forts guarding the entrance to the Dardanelles—a symbolic attack that did little actual damage.

Britain and France's Failed Assault

After months of planning, but with significant disagreement remaining about objectives, Britain and France launched a **naval attack** on the Dardanelles on March 18, 1915. A fleet led by sixteen British and French battleships attempted to force its way into the strait, with the goal of opening it by bombarding the dozens of Turkish coastal forts along the way. Although minesweeping ships had been sent ahead to clear a path, five battleships were either sunk or disabled by mines. With about one-third of the British and French battleships lost before the attack was even under way, the remaining ships were pulled back. Allied military commanders changed their objectives and decided instead to send ground forces to take over the **Gallipoli Peninsula** bordering the northern side of the strait.

The Invasion of Gallipoli

After a delay of more than a month, Allied troops—including major contingents from **Australia** and **New Zealand**—launched this ground attack, aiming to take Gallipoli completely, using ground forces. The invasion began on April 25, 1915, and the landing proceeded with relative ease. The first Turkish regiments the Allied forces encountered quickly fled the scene, making it seem as if the invasion would be an easy one.

As it turned out, the invasion was far from easy. Turkish forces returned in overwhelming numbers and pushed the Allied troops back to the beaches, where they were trapped with their backs to the sea. They remained entrenched on the beaches until January of the next year, when Britain finally pulled out in defeat. The battle raged for the entire time, with neither side making significant headway, and with losses on both sides in the hundreds of thousands.

Mesopotamia

Meanwhile, a second struggle between the British and the Turks ensued at the opposite end of the Ottoman Empire, this time for control of the oil fields of **Mesopotamia**. On November 5, 1914, a force of British and Indian soldiers launched an attack on the major Ottoman port of **Basra**. They quickly secured not only the port but also the oil fields and pipeline at **Abadan**, which had been one of the key objectives of the invasion.

Later, in early 1915, at the same time that battles were raging in Gallipoli, British forces in the Persian Gulf, under the command of General **Charles Townshend**, began advancing northward up the Tigris and Euphrates rivers with the eventual goal of seizing **Baghdad**. On June 3, 1915, they captured the Turkish garrison of **Amara** with unexpected ease—the entire garrison surrendered without a fight. On June 27, in a much more difficult battle, the British attacked **Nasariya**.

Continuing north in the unbearable heat, the Allied forces marched onward to **Kut**, which they reached and occupied on September 28. On November 22, they reached **Ctesiphon**, only twenty miles from Baghdad. At this point, however, the Turks put up a vigorous fight, and the Allied troops were forced to retreat all the way back to Kut, where they dug in. The Turks followed and lay siege to Townshend's troops at Kut for the next five months. On April 29, 1916, Townshend surrendered all 10,000 of his surviving men—the largest surrender of British troops in history up to that time.

A Two-Front War for Britain

At the start of World War I, British leaders were aware that the Ottoman Empire was slowly falling apart and thus did not regard Turkey as a serious opponent. As a result, Britain expected quick victories in both the Dardanelles and in Mesopotamia—victories that Britain needed badly in light of the gridlocked trench wars on the western front. When Turkey also became a quagmire, it was a heavy blow for Britain and sent large ripples through the government and military leadership, even costing Winston Churchill his job as first lord of the British Admiralty. Though British military leaders did have the advantage of being able to recruit forces from the many nations in its empire, the situation in Turkey and Mesopotamia left Britain facing a war on multiple fronts.

The War of Attrition in Europe

Events	
April 26, 1915	Italy signs secret "London Pact"
May 23	Italy declares war on Austria-Hungary
February 21, 1916	Battle of Verdun begins
July 1	Battle of the Somme begins
August 18	Romania signs treaty with Allied Powers
August 27	Romania declares war on Austria-Hungary, invades Transylvania
September 1	Bulgaria declares war on Romania
September 5	Bulgarian invasion of Romania reaches Danube just south of Bucharest
November 18	Battles of Verdun, the Somme end
June 7, 1917	Battle of Messines Ridge
July 2	Greece declares war on Central Powers
July 31	Battle of Passchendaele begins
November 6	Canadian forces capture Passchendaele

Italian Neutrality

Prior to the summer of 1914, **Italy** had been an ally of **Germany** and **Austria-Hungary**, as a member of the so-called **Triple Alliance** since 1882. When war broke out, however, Italy declared itself neutral and remained strictly so until the spring of 1915. All this time, Italy watched the war develop and calculated how to reap the greatest benefit from the situation.

The London Pact

In April 1915, Italy approached Austria-Hungary and offered its alliance to the **Central Powers** in exchange for a list of a half-dozen territories under Austrian control. When Austria refused a few days later, Italy turned to the **Allied Powers** with an even longer list of demands. Negotiations began immediately, and a few weeks later, on April 26, a secret agreement was signed that came to be known as the **London Pact**. The pact granted Italy claims to territories in Austria-Hungary, as well as in Albania, Turkey, and North Africa. Thus, on May 23, 1915, Italy declared war on Austria-Hungary.

South Tyrol and the Battle of Caporetto

Italian forces promptly advanced into the mountainous border regions of **South Tyrol** and to the **Isonzo River**. They made good progress at first, but within weeks, the front bogged down in the treacherous terrain, while the Austro-Hungarian forces pulled off a very effective defense. As a result, one more entrenched front line was added to the war.

The Italians and Austrians fought battle after battle along the Isonzo River, and though losses were huge, progress by either side was negligible. The situation continued largely unchanged until the Italians were defeated in the disastrous **Battle of Caporetto** in October 1917 and forced to retreat from the area. A combined total of 750,000 casualties were lost on both sides during two and a half years of fighting in which nothing substantial was accomplished.

The Battle of Verdun

During the stalemate between Italy and Austria-Hungary, one of the longest and most catastrophic battles of the war was fought several hundred miles away, in France. On February 21, 1916, Germany launched an offensive against the fortified French town of **Verdun,** which guarded the approach to Paris. The Germans intended to make a sustained attack that would drain the enemy of soldiers and force a break in the stalemate. Both sides employed shells filled with **poison gas** on a large scale. France temporarily lost Verdun and its two forts but regained the forts by battle's end and recaptured the town in a renewed attack that ended the battle on December 18. After ten months, the fighting ceased, with both sides back where they had started but with a staggering 650,000 soldiers dead. The **Battle of Verdun** was the longest single battle of the war, and among the deadliest.

The Battle of the Somme

On July 1, 1916, even as the fight was still raging at Verdun, Allied Powers launched an offensive of their own along a twenty-five-mile front that extended across both banks of the **river Somme**. The opening artillery barrage was so heavy that it could be heard in southern England. During the four-and-a-half-month **Battle of the Somme,** the Allies managed to make a small advance of only six miles, at a cost of 146,000 lives. The German death toll was 164,000.

The Stalemates in Europe

By 1916, all of the initial fronts of the war had reached stalemates, with both sides embedded in trenches and neither side gaining or losing much ground. All the while, soldiers were dying in massive numbers, simply for the sake of maintaining the status quo. The conflict was becoming a **war of attrition**, a gruesome contest to see which country could afford to lose the most soldiers. It was made all the more horrible by the fact that Britain, France, and Germany relied heavily upon their **colonies** to bolster their supplies of fighting men. Of the major participants, only Russia and later the United States relied solely upon their own populations to fight the war.

Modern Weapons and the War of Attrition

The primary reason that World War I became a war of attrition was the use of **modern weapons**. Machine guns made it easy to cut down large numbers of men quickly if they came out into the open to fight. Once opposing armies became entrenched, long-range artillery, aerial bombs, and poison gas were used to try to force the other side to abandon its shelters and retreat.

Developments in Eastern Europe

While stalemates persisted in France and South Tyrol, the situation changed in eastern Europe, where several other nations joined the war. First was **Romania**, which had remained neutral for the first two years of the war but on August 18, 1916, signed a secret pact with the **Allied Powers** granting it the right to seize the territories of Transylvania, Bukovina, and Banat in exchange for entering the war on the Allied side. Shortly thereafter, on August 27, Romania declared war on Austria-Hungary and quickly moved forces across the border into **Transylvania** (then a part of Austria-Hungary).

The situation soon became more complicated when **Bulgaria** declared war on Romania on September 1. Bulgaria promptly followed up on its declaration: on September 5, Bulgarian forces, reinforced by German and Austrian troops, attacked the Romanians at the fortress of **Tutracaia** and succeeded in capturing 25,000 prisoners of war. The struggle continued for several months, but on December 6, 1916, German troops captured Bucharest.

Several months later, on June 27, 1917, **Greece** entered the war on the side of the Allied Powers, following the abdication of Greece's pro-German king, **Constantine I**. Though Greece had been neutral through most of the war, it was surrounded by conflicts on all sides. While the king supported Germany, the government and a large portion of the population were sympathetic to the Allied Powers.

The Battle of Messines Ridge

Finally, in the summer of 1917, the British made the first small steps toward breaking the stalemate on the western front. At 3:10 A.M. on June 7, 1917, a series of simultaneous explosions ripped with amazing force through **Messines Ridge** in northern France—a fortified position along the front, where German forces had been entrenched for a long time. More than 10,000 German soldiers died instantly; those who survived were severely stunned and had no idea what had happened. Around them were craters of more than 400 feet in diameter. Before the Germans could regain their senses, the British army was upon them. Some 7,300 Germans were taken prisoner, while the rest retreated in shock.

For eighteen months prior, British soldiers had been digging a series of twenty-two tunnels below the German position. The tunnels extended up to 2,000 feet in length, and some were as far as 100 feet below the surface of the ridge where the Germans were dug in. Once complete, the tunnels were filled with 1 million pounds of high explosive and plugged with sandbags. The blast was heard as far away as London.

Slow British Progress in France

Although the Battle of Messines Ridge was a relatively small battle, it had considerable psychological impact for both sides. It also broke the Germans' hold on the ridge, forcing them to retreat eastward and marking the beginning of a slow but continuous loss of ground by German forces in the west. After the battle, British forces continued to push the Germans back a few hundred yards at a time toward the high ridge at **Passchendaele**. The Germans fought back with **mustard gas**, a notoriously slow-acting chemical agent that maimed or killed enemy soldiers via severe blisters on the skin or internally if breathed.

The Battle of Passchendaele

By mid-September 1917, the British, close to their goal, began a new offensive movement. The fighting was slow and exhausting, and even the slightest forward progress came with innumerable casualties. The British reached Passchendaele on October 12 during a driving rain that turned the landscape to impenetrable mud. During the **Battle of Passchendaele** that ensued, the British suffered 310,000 casualties, while German casualties numbered 260,000. The battle proved the last great battle of attrition on the western front and again saw the use of mustard gas and other deadly chemical weapons.

THE UNITED STATES ENTERS THE WAR

EVENTS

October 21, 1916	French renew attack on Verdun
November 7	Wilson reelected on antiwar platform; begins diplomatic initiatives
February 1, 1917	Germany begins unrestricted submarine warfare
February 3	German U-boat sinks U.S. cargo ship *Housatonic* United States breaks off diplomatic relations with Germany
February 24	United States learns of Zimmermann telegram
March 1	Zimmermann telegram published in American press
April 2	Wilson asks Congress to declare war
April 6	United States declares war on Germany
May 24	First U.S. convoy to protect shipping to Europe departs
July 4	U.S. troops march through central Paris to Lafayette's tomb
September 4	First U.S. war fatalities
November 2–3	First U.S. combat mission
January 8, 1918	Wilson gives "Fourteen Points" speech before U.S. Congress

KEY PEOPLE

David Lloyd George	British prime minister during the war; rejected Wilson's peace initiatives in 1916
John J. Pershing	Commander of U.S. forces deployed in Europe
Woodrow Wilson	U.S. president during the war; attempted to maintain neutrality but saw it crumble in 1917
Alfred Zimmermann	German foreign minister; sent telegram attempting to incite Mexico to attack the United States

SUMMARY & ANALYSIS

AMERICAN NEUTRALITY

Since the beginning of World War I in 1914, the **United States**, under President **Woodrow Wilson**, had maintained strict neutrality, other than providing material assistance to the Allies. Even in May 1915, when a German submarine sank the British ocean liner ***Lusitania***, killing 128 U.S. citizens out of a total 1,200 dead, the United States, though in uproar, remained neutral. In the autumn of 1916, Wilson was reelected after running largely on a platform of antiwar, pro-neutrality rhetoric.

AMERICAN DIPLOMACY

By the time of Wilson's reelection victory, the war had left millions dead, cities and economies in ruins, and no decisive victory in sight for any side. It seemed that the war might actually burn itself out. In November and December 1916, Wilson began a series of initiatives to broker a resolution, sending out diplomatic notes to the governments of every nation involved. Germany responded positively and went so far as to recommend opening immediate peace negotiations. France, however, responded by launching a renewed attack against the Germans in Verdun. British prime minister **David Lloyd George** rejected Wilson's initiative directly.

Unrestricted Submarine Warfare

In January 1917, Germany announced that it would lift all restrictions on **submarine warfare** starting on February 1. This declaration meant that German U-boat commanders were suddenly authorized to sink all ships that they believed to be providing aid of any sort to the Allies. Because the primary goal was to starve Britain into surrendering, the German effort would focus largely on ships crossing the Atlantic from the United States and Canada.

The Housatonic

The first victim of this new policy was the American cargo ship ***Housatonic***, which a German U-boat sank on February 3, 1917. In response, President Wilson broke off diplomatic relations with Germany the same day. The escalation was serious and turned out to be a major step toward the United States' entry into the war.

The Zimmermann Telegram

In the meantime, other German mischief paved the road to war with the United States even more smoothly. In February 1917, British intelligence intercepted a telegram from Germany that they had intercepted in January. In the telegram, sent by German foreign minister **Alfred Zimmermann** to his ambassador in **Mexico** on January 16, Zimmermann instructed the ambassador to offer Mexico generous financial aid if it would ally itself with Germany against the United States. Furthermore, the telegram promised German support for Mexico in reconquering its lost territory in Texas, New Mexico, and Arizona.

On March 1, 1917, the text of the **Zimmermann telegram** appeared on the front pages of American newspapers, and in a heartbeat, American public opinion shifted in favor of entering the war.

The U.S. Declaration of War

Although Wilson tried hard to keep the United States neutral, by the spring of 1917, the situation had changed significantly, and neutrality no longer seemed feasible. Germany's unrestricted submarine warfare was taking its toll, as American ships, both cargo and passenger, were sunk one after another. The exposure of the Zimmermann telegram and other German subterfuge further convinced the American public that the war was threatening American interests. Finally, on April 2, Wilson appeared before Congress and requested a declaration of war. Congress responded within days, officially declaring war on Germany on April 6, 1917.

The Convoy System

By the time the United States entered the war, German submarines were causing catastrophic damage to the supply of food and other resources coming into Britain from abroad. On May 24, 1917, the British admiralty finally gave in to demands to establish a system of **convoys**. Under the plan, British warships would provide heavily armed escorts for all ships coming to Britain from the United States, Canada, and other countries. The plan was especially important from the U.S. perspective, as American soldiers would soon begin heading to Britain by ship in large numbers. More than half a dozen convoy gathering points were soon established along the North American coast.

The convoys had an immediate and dramatic effect. The number of ships, supplies, and men lost to German submarines plummeted, virtually nullifying Germany's effort to force Britain's surrender. There was a downside, however, as it meant that Britain now had far fewer naval assets available to protect its coast or to engage the German navy at sea.

Arrival of U.S. Troops in Europe

All through the summer of 1917, U.S. troops were ferried across the Atlantic, first to Britain and then on to France, where they came under the leadership of General **John J. Pershing**. The first public display of the troops came on July 4, when a large U.S. detachment held a symbolic march through Paris to the grave of the Marquis de Lafayette, the French aristocrat who had fought alongside the United States during the American Revolution.

First U.S. Combat Involvement

Though U.S. leaders had not planned major military involvement until the summer of 1918, some forces saw combat in the fall of 1917. The first American fatalities on the ground in Europe occurred on September 4, when four soldiers were killed during a German air raid. The first full-fledged combat involving U.S. troops happened on November 2–3, 1917, at Bathelémont, France; three were killed and twelve were taken as German prisoners of war.

Wilson's Fourteen Points

On January 8, 1918, President Wilson gave a speech before the U.S. Congress in which he defined a total of fourteen distinct requirements that he saw as necessary in order to restore and maintain peace in Europe and the rest of the world. The requirements soon came to be known simply as Wilson's **"Fourteen Points."**

Some of these points—such as the evacuation of German troops from Russia, France, and Belgium—were basic steps necessary for ending hostilities; other points were part of a long-range vision for preventing future conflicts. Among these long-term points was a suggestion that diplomacy and treaties always be carried out openly and in full public view. Wilson further suggested that all economic barriers be eliminated and that all nations adopt an "equality of trading conditions." The final, fourteenth point called for establishing a **"general association"** of the world's states, with each to have equal representation regardless of size or strength. Although the details of Wilson's plan would be adjusted considerably over time, his proposals laid the foundation for the armistice negotiations that would take place ten months later.

Assessing the U.S. Entrance

In the year leading up to the U.S. declaration of war, President Wilson's position on the war changed dramatically. Although the United States had long maintained a much warmer relationship with Great Britain and France than with Germany or Austria-Hungary, Wilson's administration kept a strictly neutral stance. Moreover, as Wilson began making diplomatic initiatives in 1916, his position toward the Central Powers was considerably more lenient than the Allies were comfortable with.

This evenhanded diplomacy evaporated quickly, however, when Germany lifted its restrictions on submarine warfare in January 1917. Although it was the Zimmermann telegram that effectively turned American public opinion, in truth, the "threat" presented in the telegram bordered on the absurd. The threat from German submarines, on the other hand, was a direct threat to American lives, commerce, and property and had to be countered. There could now be little question of the United States remaining neutral, and within two months, the United States declared war.

At it turned out, there was a large time gap between the U.S. declaration of war and the actual entrance of U.S. troops in combat on the front. The U.S. Army was not the vast and flexible force that it is today, and much time would be needed for large numbers of U.S. soldiers to be trained, moved into place, and organized. Even after troops were finally in combat, the United States never formally joined the Allied forces but technically remained an independent participant, at war only with Germany and not with Austria-Hungary.

Russia Exits the War

Events	
March 8, 1917	Riots in Petrograd develop into the beginning of the February Revolution
March 15	Tsar Nicholas II abdicates
April 16	Lenin arrives in Petrograd from Germany
July 1	New Russian offensive opens on eastern front Antiwar riot in Petrograd
November 6–7	Bolshevik (October) Revolution
November 8	Lenin declares peace, though sporadic fighting continues
November 26	Bolsheviks call for end to hostilities on all fronts
December 15	Russian cease-fire declared

Note: All dates are according to the modern, Gregorian calendar instead of the Julian calendar that was used in Russia at the time.

Key People	
Alexander Kerensky	Russian minister of war who led the provisional government after the tsar's abdication
Vladimir Lenin	Bolshevik revolutionary who seized power in November 1917 and declared Russia to be at peace
Nicholas II	Russian tsar who lost power in the revolutions of 1917

A Costly War for Russia

Over the first two and a half years of the war, **Russia** had experienced heavy defeats against Germany but at the same time had significant successes against Austria-Hungary. In any case, however, the war had become hugely unpopular at home. The Russian death toll was enormous, Russia was continuously losing territory, and the war had sparked food shortages throughout the country. Although there was a certain level of popular sympathy for Serbia, most Russians felt that the country had little to gain in the war and much to lose.

Popular confidence in Tsar **Nicholas II** was also at an all-time low. Not only was the tsar out of touch with the people, but many felt he had become a puppet, either of his German-born wife or of various special-interest groups. Although Russia was hardly a democracy, public opinion was still a powerful factor. Numerous underground organizations had sprung up over the previous few decades to oppose the tsar and his policies. More recently, labor strikes had begun wreaking havoc upon Russian industry.

The February Revolution

In early March 1917 (late February by the Julian calendar in use in Russia at the time), the tsar's entire regime unexpectedly collapsed after a series of large demonstrations in the Russian capital of **Petrograd.** Under pressure from both the military and the parliament, Nicholas II abdicated on March 15 (modern calendar). The event became known as the **February Revolution.**

As the struggle for control of the country began, parts of the military continued to fight on the war front, others quit fighting altogether, and others even fought each other. Germany quickly recognized an opportunity and made arrangements to help Russian revolutionaries in Europe, including **Vladimir Lenin**, to get back to Russia in order to fuel the ensuing chaos there. Lenin arrived in Petrograd on April 16 on a train provided by Germany.

The Last Russian Offensive

After the developments of March 1917, participants on all sides watched Russia closely to see what it would do without a tsar. Although a new provisional government was officially in charge, the situation in Russia remained highly unstable, especially in the military. On July 1, Russian forces opened several new offensives along the eastern front—an action that Russian minister of war **Alexander Kerensky** ordered as part of an effort to boost morale in the army. On the same day, however, a huge antiwar rally clogged the streets of Petrograd.

Although the Russian advances initially showed promise against Austrian forces in Galicia, the Russian troops fled quickly when German reinforcements arrived. Sporadic fighting along the eastern front continued throughout July and August, but growing desertions, infighting, and general disorder throughout the Russian military greatly diminished its effectiveness over time.

The Bolshevik Revolution

Russia's position in the war remained in question throughout the summer and fall of 1917. Officially, the country was still at war, and fighting did continue. However, there was intense disagreement in the country over whether or not Russia should remain at war, and if not, under what conditions it should leave the conflict.

The provisional government, under the leadership of Alexander Kerensky, favored remaining in the war until Germany and Austria-Hungary were defeated. The more radical **Petrograd Soviet**, a loose conglomeration of labor unions with a largely Socialist/Communist leadership, felt that Russia should get out of the war as soon as possible but also recognized that pulling out immediately would likely mean a loss of territory and heavy reparations. A third group, the **Bolsheviks**, who had even more radical leanings than the Petrograd Soviet, wanted the country to exit the war immediately, no matter the cost.

The debate continued throughout the summer and fall until November 6, 1917 (October 24 by the Russian calendar). On that day, the Bolsheviks seized total control of the country with the help of the military. The next day, Bolshevik leader Vladimir Lenin issued his first decree, declaring Russia to be at peace. Though he ordered the Russian military to cease all hostilities, the country's formal exit from the war would be somewhat more complicated.

Russia's Cease-Fire

On November 26, 1917, the Bolsheviks issued a call for a halt to hostilities on all fronts and requested that all sides immediately make arrangements to sign an armistice. This idea was not well received by France and Britain, who still intended to push the Germans out of their lands. When Russia received no response, it made another call, warning that if no one responded, Russia would make a **separate peace**. When there still was no response, the Bolsheviks, in an effort to embarrass the Allied forces, published a series of secret treaties that Russia had made with the Allies.

After several days of negotiations, a **cease-fire** was declared on December 15, 1917. A formal peace treaty, however, proved more difficult to achieve. It took months of negotiations, and Russia lost an enormous amount of territory. Russia's land losses included Finland, Poland, Latvia, Lithuania, Estonia, the Ukraine, Belarus, Bessarabia, and the Caucasus region, along with some of the coal-mining regions of southern Russia.

The Fallout from Russia's Exit

Russia's departure from the war posed a serious danger to the Allied forces, for it effectively closed the eastern front and thus meant that the Allies would soon face some 900,000 additional German troops on the western front. In addition, the large quantities of Russian equipment that the Germans captured would also now be used on the Allies. The United States provided the only possible hope to counter this sudden turning of the tables, but U.S. forces were not expected to begin major combat operations until the summer of 1918. On the whole, one might argue that Russia's pullout, rather than bring the world closer to peace, likely extended the conflict by enabling Germany and Austria-Hungary to focus their entire attention on the west and south.

For Russia itself, the exit from the war cost most of the territorial gains the country had made since the reign of Peter the Great in the early 1700s. Although the Bolsheviks pronounced themselves Russia's new leaders, their practical control extended little beyond Petrograd and Moscow. The war had drained Russia: 1.7 million of its soldiers had died in battle, and 3 million Russian civilians had perished as well. Moreover, the country was left in chaos, as there were still large groups of people remaining in Russia who opposed the Bolsheviks' rule. Some sought to bring back the tsar; others favored a democratic government akin to the one promised by the provisional government that the Bolsheviks had overthrown. In the end, though Russia got out of World War I, the civil war that soon started within the country turned out to be even more costly for its people than World War I had been.

Endgame

Events	
March 21, 1918	Germany launches spring offensive
March 23	German long-range guns begin shelling Paris
March 24	German forces cross the Somme
March 25	Allied front line is broken
March 30	Germans are stopped at Moreuil Wood
April 9–29	Battle of Lys
May 2	General Pershing compromises on sending U.S. troops to the front
May 7	Romania signs peace treaty with Central Powers
May 12	Germany and Austria sign pact to exploit the Ukraine
May 21	Mutinies begin in Austrian army
May 28	U.S. victory at Cantigny
July 18	Allies begin major counteroffensive
July 26	Allies foil German attack at Château-Thierry
September 19	Turkey defeated at Megiddo

Germany's Push for Paris

With its newly arrived forces from the eastern front, **Germany** enjoyed superiority in numbers on the western front for the first time since the earliest days of the war. Nonetheless, all sides, including Germany, were exhausted. Their strength was limited, and fresh troops from the United States would soon be ready to join the fight on the Allied side. If Germany was going to somehow win the war, now was the time.

Germany therefore poured all of its remaining resources into a massive offensive that began in the early morning hours of March 21, 1918. The goal was to push across the river Somme and then on to **Paris**. Like most land battles in World War I, the offensive began with a prolonged artillery barrage. In this case it lasted for five hours and included a heavy concentration of **poison gas** shells along with the usual explosive ordinance. When the German troops moved forward through a combination of heavy fog and poison gas clouds, visibility was near zero, and soldiers on both sides were largely unable to distinguish friendly from enemy forces. By midday, the fog had lifted, and a furious air battle took place over the soldiers' heads while the Germans relentlessly pounded the Allies.

As the Germans surged forward, they brought with them the newest long-range **artillery cannons** developed by Krupp, which enabled them to fire accurately upon Paris from the astounding range of seventy-four miles. On March 23, these shells killed more than 250 unsuspecting Parisians, who were baffled because they initially thought the blasts were coming from the ground. The long-distance German shells killed hundreds more in the following days. On March 24, the Germans raced across the Somme, having captured the bridges before the French could destroy them. On March 25, the Allied front broke at precisely the point where the French and British troop lines met.

The Battle of Lys

German momentum continued for another five days until a British advance halted the Germans at **Moreuil Wood** on March 30. The Allies pushed the Germans back for several days more, until the initiative was turned around once more at the **Battle of Lys**, which began on April 9, 1918. At Lys, the British and French began to lose ground once more, and the Germans recaptured places (such as Passchendaele and Messines) that the Allies had won in hard-fought battles the previous year.

By the end of the Battle of Lys on April 29, the German army, despite its run of recent success, saw morale at an all-time low. The French and British were in almost as bad a state. During this period of the war, whenever either side launched an offensive, it would only last a few days before the troops ran out of energy and began to fall back. Nonetheless, neither British, nor French, nor German leaders would give up, so the war continued in this way for much of the summer.

Delays in the U.S. Deployment

Only the **United States**, it seemed, held the power to shift the balance, but more than a year had passed since the U.S. declaration of war, with little tangible result. Although hundreds of thousands of American troops had been transported to Europe, very few of them had actually participated in combat.

Britain and France wanted the U.S. troops to be integrated into their own armies and sent to the front to fight, but the U.S. government insisted that its troops would fight only as an independent army under U.S. commanders. Because this setup would take a long time to organize in an overseas environment, the policy drew bitter criticism from the French and British, who were still fighting the brunt of the war. The official U.S. entrance into the war in 1917 had given the Allies hope in the face of Russia's exit. But in light of the slow pace of actual U.S. entry, many in France and Britain feared that they might lose the war before the American troops ever fired a shot.

At a meeting of the Supreme War Council of Allied Leaders on May 2, 1918, there was a small shift in the U.S. stance. General **John J. Pershing**, the commander of American forces in Europe, agreed to a compromise, pledging to send 130,000 troops that month and several hundred thousand more in the coming months to fight on the front with the French and British forces. This commitment mean that roughly one-third of the American forces present in Europe would see action that summer. U.S. leaders estimated that the rest, however, would not be organized, trained, and ready to fight until the late spring of 1919.

Turmoil in the East

Although Russia was fully out of the war, much unfinished business remained in the territories along the old **eastern front**. On May 7, 1918, **Romania** signed a peace treaty with the Central Powers, giving up control of the mouth of the Danube River along the Black Sea coast. At the same time, German troops advanced to the southeast, through the Ukraine, southern Russia, and on to the Caucasus region. The **Bolsheviks** still did not have an effective hold on this region, so the Germans were able to proceed largely unchallenged.

On May 12, Germany and Austria-Hungary signed an agreement to share in reaping economic benefits from the Ukraine. Barely a week later, however, Austria-Hungary experienced the first in a series of **mutinies** in its army, carried out by nationalist groups. The first mutiny involved a group of Slovenes; almost as soon as it was suppressed, other mutinies broke out, led in turn by Serbs, Rusyns (Ruthenians), and Czechs.

The Influenza Outbreak

During the summer of 1918, an unusually severe strain of **influenza** spread rapidly around the world. Although influenza was not normally associated with high mortality rates, this strain was especially virulent, and it would eventually kill millions of people.

The cause of the outbreak is unknown, but the war was most certainly a contributing factor. First, the war encouraged large-scale movements of people back and forth around the globe, which accelerated the spread of the virus. Second, it is thought that the numerous war-ravaged regions of the world experienced poorer nutrition and less sanitary conditions, leaving their populations especially susceptible.

At the same time, the spread of the disease directly affected the war itself. All sides lost soldiers to the flu outbreak, but Germany and Austria-Hungary were hit especially hard, with the armies of both countries becoming severely weakened just as the Allies were beginning to take the offensive. The epidemic continued well into 1919, when it suddenly died out just as quickly as it had started.

Cantigny: The First American Victory

By the end of May 1918, several thousand American troops had appeared on the front ready to fight, arriving just in time to meet the latest German offensive. The U.S. forces were involved in several battles, most notably at **Cantigny**, on the Somme. Here, 4,000 American soldiers attacked German forces on May 28, while the French provided cover with tanks, airplanes, and artillery. They successfully liberated the town of Cantigny and then held the line during three successive days of German counterattacks. U.S. forces suffered over 1,000 casualties during the engagement.

The Allied Counteroffensive

Throughout June and early July 1918, the Germans attempted a series of offensive actions, still trying to break through the Allied defense lines in France. The lines held, however, in part due to the newly provided American reinforcements.

On June 3, a German attack at **Château-Thierry** was stymied by intelligence that the Allies gained from German prisoners of war. Knowing of the German plans in advance, the French created a false front line, complete with trenches. The German artillery barrage ended up landing on a set of trenches that were largely empty, and when the German soldiers rushed forward, they found themselves facing mostly fresh and unfazed Allied soldiers who opened fire upon them, leaving the Germans in disarray. Nonetheless, the Germans continued the attack over the next two days, once again threatening Paris.

The Allies responded on June 6 with a counterattack of their own, using combined forces from France, Britain, Italy, and the United States. The attack was devastating, killing over 30,000 German soldiers in twenty days. Although the battle continued for many weeks, the Germans' will to fight was shattered, and Kaiser **Wilhelm II** knew that the end was looming. German troops were losing ground every day, and the Allies intensified their attacks with every opportunity. The momentum stayed with them, and they steadily drove the Germans back during all of August and September.

Turkey in Retreat

In the Near East, meanwhile, the tide had turned in the war with the **Ottoman Empire** since the devastating British defeats in Gallipoli and Mesopotamia back in 1916. Since then, Britain had captured **Baghdad** along with all of **Mesopotamia**. Farther south, on the **Arabian Peninsula**, revolts by desert tribesmen had broken Turkey's long-lasting grip on the region.

In December 1917, the British captured the city of **Jerusalem** in Palestine and slowly began advancing toward Turkey proper. Finally, on September 19, 1918, the British launched a direct attack on the Turkish front at **Megiddo** and won a major victory that forced the Turks into a full-scale retreat. By mid-October, Turkey was asking for peace terms.

The Final Phase of Combat

Although this final period of major combat saw two major developments—the Russian exit and the U.S. entrance—the degree to which these events impacted the war is debatable. By the spring of 1918, both sides' armies were exhausted from years of fighting and had little reason to hope that an end would soon come. While there were some hints of peace discussions late in the summer, the political and military leaders of all the remaining warring countries were actively planning combat operations intended to last well into 1919.

Russia's exit from the war gave the Germans a renewed hope of achieving victory, just as the appearance of American troops in Europe gave similar hope to the French and British; however, neither of these events really turned the tide. Rather, they effectively balanced each other out, while the catastrophic influenza outbreak placed a heavy burden on both sides. Ultimately, the real trigger for the end of the war appears to have come from the mass mutinies within the Austro-Hungarian and German militaries.

The Collapse of the Central Powers

Events	
September 29, 1918	Wilhelm II pressured into accepting parliamentary government Bulgaria surrenders, signs armistice
October 3	Wilhelm II hands Parliament authority on military decisions Prince Max von Baden named chancellor of Germany
October 7	Poland declares itself an independent state
October 12	Germany agrees to withdraw forces from France, Belgium
October 14	Provisional government formed in Czechoslovakia Ottoman sultan requests peace terms for Turkey
October 25	Hungarian National Council established in Budapest Allied leaders meet at Senlis to establish formal armistice terms
October 29	Yugoslavia proclaims itself an independent state
October 30	Germany announces end to submarine warfare Turkey signs armistice
November 3	Austria signs armistice, begins to withdraw forces
November 9	German delegation begins formal armistice negotiations at Compiègne Max von Baden announces abdication of Wilhelm II
November 11	Germany signs armistice, formally ending the war
June 28, 1919	Treaty of Versailles signed

Germany and Austria Surrounded

By October 1918, although France and Belgium were still far from being free of German troops, it was clear to all sides that the **western front** was slowly collapsing. At the same time, Allied forces were steadily advancing northward from the south, liberating much of **Serbia** and putting pressure upon Austria-Hungary. Neither Germany nor Austria-Hungary was yet ready to surrender, but Germany's government was undergoing a revolution, and Austria-Hungary's army was collapsing amid mass mutiny.

Revolution in Germany

Germany's first **revolution** was a quiet one that happened in two stages. On September 29, 1918, Germany's top two generals, **Paul von Hindenburg** and **Erich Ludendorff**, pressured Kaiser **Wilhelm II** into establishing a constitutional monarchy, because the Allied forces refused to negotiate with the kaiser and insisted upon dealing with representatives of the German people instead.

On October 2, the kaiser relinquished all of his authority regarding military decisions to the new **Parliament**—an act that, for all practical purposes, reduced the kaiser to a figurehead. His cousin,

Prince **Max von Baden**, was named chancellor and effectively assumed leadership of the country. Although Prince Max immediately began to make inquiries to the Allies about an armistice, he was not ready to surrender unconditionally, as he believed that he could negotiate favorable terms for Germany, despite continuing losses on the battlefield. A lengthy exchange of diplomatic notes went on for the next month.

Independence in Eastern Europe

Bulgaria was the first of the Central Powers to surrender, signing an armistice in Salonica on September 29, 1918. On October 7, **Poland** declared itself an independent state, which immediately sparked fighting between Poland and **Ukraine** over the possession of the border territory of East Galicia. On October 14, the provisional government of **Czechoslovakia** came into existence. On October 25, a Hungarian National Council was established in Budapest in preparation for an independent **Hungary**, separate from Austria.

The Elusive Peace

As the war petered out, President **Woodrow Wilson** of the United States became the primary Allied representative for handling the peace negotiations. Earlier in the war, when the United States was neutral, Wilson had repeatedly attempted to broker peace among the fighting powers and made sincere efforts to work out an agreement that would be fair to all sides. By 1918, however, Wilson's position had changed considerably. American soldiers were now fighting and dying against the Germans in France, and both Germany and Austria had considerably less leverage than before. Wilson was now determined that neither country would gain peace cheaply.

The Central Powers' Attempts at Diplomacy

On October 3–4, 1918, the first **joint German-Austrian diplomatic note** was sent to Wilson, requesting an armistice and suggesting that all hostilities end without any penalties for either side. Wilson rejected the note on October 8, stating that he would not even discuss the idea of an armistice until France, Belgium, and Serbia were completely free of German and Austrian forces.

On October 12, the German government announced that it had accepted Wilson's requirement and that it would **withdraw its forces** from France and Belgium. Despite the announcement, however, the fighting on the western front continued without letup.

On October 21, Germany announced that it would **cease all submarine warfare**. On October 25, Allied military commanders met at **Senlis**, France, to discuss formal terms for an armistice. Although they disagreed over matters of detail, all concurred that Germany must be rendered unable to make war again.

The Dissolution of Austria-Hungary

By the end of October, Germany was still actively trying to broker a favorable way out of the war, but **Austria** could no longer afford to wait, because the country was already falling apart. On October 27, 1918, Austria approached the Allies independently for an armistice and ordered the Austrian army to retreat the same day. On October 29, Serbs, Croats, and Slovenes proclaimed the establishment of a southern Slavic state to be called **Yugoslavia**.

On October 30, an Austrian delegation arrived in Italy to surrender unconditionally. That same day, **Hungary** formally declared its independence. On November 3, all the terms of the Austrian armistice were in place, and on the following day, Austria-Hungary formally ceased to exist.

The Collapse of the Ottoman Empire

On October 14, 1918, Sultan **Mehmed VI** of the **Ottoman Empire**, having suffered heavy territorial losses over the past year and facing a British invasion of Turkey proper, requested peace terms. An armistice was signed on October 30. One of its terms was that the **Dardanelles** be opened immediately to Allied ships. In the coming months, most of the territory of the Ottoman Empire would be redistributed under the trusteeship of various Allied forces and eventually reorganized into independent countries.

The Collapse of Germany

In the early days of November 1918, the situation in Germany deteriorated from unstable to outright chaotic. Prince **Max von Baden** proved ineffective at negotiating favorable terms for a German armistice, and unrest within the military grew, especially in the navy, where mutinies were becoming widespread. Kaiser **Wilhelm II**, who by this point was in hiding in the Belgian resort town of **Spa**, found himself under rapidly increasing pressure to abdicate, which he stubbornly refused to do.

On November 7, Max dispatched a group of German delegates by train to the secluded location of **Compiègne**, France, to negotiate an armistice. The delegation arrived on the morning of November 9, and negotiation promptly began. That same day, Prince Max took the step of announcing Wilhelm II's **abdication** of the German throne—without the now-delusional kaiser's agreement. Prince Max himself then resigned, and separate left-wing political groups respectively proclaimed the establishment of a **German Soviet Republic** and a **German Socialist Republic**, though neither would actually come to be.

The Armistice

Finally, on November 11, at 5:10 A.M., the **armistice with Germany** was signed. Hostilities officially ended at 11:00 A.M. that day. Thus, the end of World War I is generally reported to have come on the eleventh hour of the eleventh day of the eleventh month of 1918. It would be more than seven months, however, before formal peace treaties would finalize the arrangements among all the various warring nations.

The Treaty of Versailles

Just as it had begun, World War I ended with complicated diplomatic negotiations. It took many months, but the treaty defining Germany's present and future existence was signed at **Versailles** on June 28, 1919.

For Germany, it was a day of complete humiliation. The country was required to accept **losses of territory**, including Alsace-Lorraine and much of present-day Poland. Germany would retain the border region of the Rhineland but was strictly forbidden to develop the area militarily. Germany also had to agree to pay massive **war reparations** that would require half a century to fulfill. Finally, Germany was forced to publicly acknowledge and accept **full responsibility** for the entire war. This stipulation was a hard pill for many Germans to swallow, and indeed it was a blatant untruth.

The Legacy of the War

World War I began with a cold-blooded murder, diplomatic intrigue, and overconfident guesses about what the other side would do. Contemporary accounts report that there was even a sense of excitement and adventure in the air, as some seemed to envision the war more as a chance to try out the newest technological innovations than anything else. Five tragic years later, the reality of the war was unfathomably different: tens of millions dead, entire countries in ruins, and economies in shambles. Millions of soldiers had been drawn into the war, many from faraway colonies and many with little more than an inkling of what it was they were fighting for.

The Treaty of Versailles, rather than fix these problems, imposed bewilderingly harsh terms upon Germany, forcing that nation to accept full financial and diplomatic responsibility for the entire war. In the peace treaties ending most previous European wars, each side had accepted its losses, claimed its spoils, shaken hands, and then moved on. After World War I, however, the German people were humiliated, impoverished, and left with nothing to hope for but more of the same. Internally, Germany became a tumultuous place, teetering on the brink of violent revolutions from both the right and the left and vulnerable to takeover from extremist elements like the Nazi Party. Indeed, just a few decades would prove that the Allies had gone overboard with the punishments they inflicted on Germany—a misjudgment that created precisely the conditions required to launch Europe into the center of an even more horrible war.

Study Questions & Essay Topics

Always use specific historical examples to support your arguments.

Study Questions

1. *World War I has often been described as an "unnecessary war." Why? Do you agree?*

World War I has been called unnecessary because the original dispute that triggered the conflict was limited, yet it triggered a massive, global war. In short, the conflict stemmed merely from Austria-Hungary and Serbia's disagreement over how to handle the assassination of Archduke Ferdinand: the Austro-Hungarian government believed that the Serbian government was connected with the assassination and therefore demanded to be involved in the investigation and judicial process within Serbia. No other countries had a direct interest in the matter. Russia and Germany were the next to get involved, not because of animosity toward each other but because of their intentions to protect Serbia and Austria-Hungary, respectively. France, Britain, and the Ottoman Empire had even less interest in the matter. Thus, one could argue that much of the war could have been avoided if Russia and Germany had simply kept out of the matter.

On the other hand, real tensions existed among many of the principal nations prior to the war, and these conflicting ambitions contributed to the war's escalation. In particular, the naval arms race between Germany and Britain was intensifying, and growing German colonial ambitions raised the tension level further. Additionally, the spread of nationalism in southern Europe was destabilizing Austria-Hungary, making the country dangerously vulnerable to minority uprisings. Thus, many observers and strategists felt that an armed conflict between the European powers was inevitable; the disagreement over the archduke's assassination simply provided a spark and an outlet.

2. *What, if any, are the connections between the causes of the war in 1914 and the reasons that the war was still going on in 1918?*

In many ways, World War I in mid-1914 and World War I in mid-1918 are unrelated. What started as a local conflict over a political assassination had become an unbelievable bloodbath: the Indian troops fighting in Mesopotamia, the Australians fighting in Gallipoli, and the Americans fighting in France had little invested in the conflict between Austria-Hungary and Serbia. The same was largely true at the government level in many of the warring nations. For the Allied Powers, the fight was mostly about Germany, not Austria-Hungary. By 1918, those who were still fighting were doing so because they could not find a way to stop without facing unacceptable losses.

On the other hand, some of the roots of the original conflict—factors that predated Archduke Franz Ferdinand's assassination—were still present and still unresolved. Nationalism, which was spreading rapidly through southern and eastern Europe, became the major cause of mutinies in the Austro-Hungarian army. Ultimately, these mutinies caused Austria-Hungary's collapse, isolating Germany and helping bring about the war's end. Thus, one could argue that the same problem that had started the war was at least partly responsible for ending it.

3. *Consider the role of diplomacy in World War I. How was it a positive influence? How was it a negative one?*

Although diplomacy traditionally is used to *prevent* armed conflicts from happening, in the case of World War I, it in many ways played the opposite role, whether intended or not. Few of the combatant nations in World War I were directly interested in the disputes between Serbia and Austria-Hungary, and in many cases they became involved only because of treaties obligating them to defend other countries. Although some of these treaties were publicly known, many had been made in secret, preventing potential enemies from ascertaining the consequences of their actions.

This opaqueness of diplomacy was arguably one of the main factors that led Germany to make such aggressive moves early in the war, as many German leaders believed that Britain would never enter the war against them. Russia likewise pursued a number of secret treaties and agreements both before and during the war. Italy even went so far as to shop around secretly when trying to decide which side offered the greatest potential benefits. Ultimately, these secret diplomatic maneuverings escalated the war to catastrophic levels. As a result, one of President Wilson's Fourteen Points policy was that henceforth, all treaties and trade agreements between nations be held with full public disclosure.

Suggested Essay Topics

1. *What is trench warfare, and why was so much of World War I dominated by this method of fighting? Consider such elements as technology, strategy, attitudes of leaders, and any other factors you can think of. How did trench warfare affect the duration of the war?*

2. *After the war, Germany was punished much more severely than were the remnants of Austria-Hungary. Do you think this was reasonable? In your answer, consider the roles each country shared in starting and escalating the war. Also consider the roles of Serbia and Russia.*

3. *How did the use of new technologies during World War I influence the war? Which sides benefited the most from which technologies? Did any of them play a role in either lengthening or in shortening the war? Which technologies were the most important?*

4. *Discuss the U.S. policy on American troops serving in Europe during World War I. Why do you think American commanders were hesitant to allow U.S. soldiers to serve in British and French regiments? What effect did this policy have on America's relations with the other Allied countries?*

5. *What was the Schlieffen Plan and why was it unsuccessful during World War I?*

Review & Resources

Quiz

1. Which country made the first declaration of war?

    A. Germany
    B. Serbia
    C. Russia
    D. Austria-Hungary

2. In what city was Archduke Franz Ferdinand assassinated?

    A. Zagreb
    B. Sarajevo
    C. Belgrade
    D. Vienna

3. At the beginning of World War I, Bosnia-Herzegovina was part of

    A. Austria-Hungary
    B. Yugoslavia
    C. Serbia
    D. Croatia

4. To which other prominent leader was Kaiser Wilhelm II of Germany related?

    A. Woodrow Wilson of the United States
    B. Franz Joseph of Austria-Hungary
    C. Nicholas II of Russia
    D. Winston Churchill of Britain

5. Germany's attack upon which country directly provoked Britain to go to war?

    A. France
    B. Russia
    C. Belgium
    D. Holland

6. Germany's plan for fighting France and Russia was called

   A. The Hindenburg Plan
   B. The Schlieffen Plan
   C. Operation Barbarossa
   D. Sturm und Drang

7. What key fortress was the scene of the heaviest fighting during the German invasion of Belgium?

   A. Liege
   B. Fort Heineken
   C. The Hague
   D. Maginot

8. Which Russian general lost the Battle of the Masurian Lakes?

   A. Samsonov
   B. Kornilov
   C. Kerensky
   D. Rennenkampf

9. Which early battle marked the first major German defeat?

   A. Tannenberg
   B. The Marne
   C. Mons
   D. Masurian Lakes

10. Which best describes Austria-Hungary's progress early in the war?

   A. Defeat by Russia; defeat by Serbia
   B. Victory over Russia; defeat by Serbia
   C. Defeat by Russia; victory over Serbia
   D. Victory over Russia; victory over Serbia

11. What event prompted the Ottoman Empire to enter the war?

   A. A British attack on the Dardanelles
   B. A German attack on Russia
   C. A Russian attack on Austria
   D. A British attack on Gallipoli

12. The commander of the German East Asia Squadron was

A. Otto von Bismarck
B. Erich Ludendorff
C. Alfred von Tirpitz
D. Maximilian von Spee

13. The Battle of the Falkland Islands resulted in

A. Victory for Britain
B. Victory for Argentina
C. Victory for Germany
D. Victory for Turkey

14. Which is generally *not* true of sea warfare during World War I?

A. Submarines and mines were a cheap and effective way to threaten battleships
B. Convoys eventually proved to be the most effective defense against submarines
C. The British navy dominated the world's oceans through its aggressive use of submarine warfare
D. Great sea battles between surface ships were relatively rare during the war

15. Why did Britain need control of the Dardanelles?

A. To open shipping routes with Russia
B. To gain access to the Persian Gulf
C. To cut off German naval bases in the Black Sea
D. To prevent Russian ships from entering the Baltic Sea

16. Which was a political result of Britain's invasion of Gallipoli?

A. Winston Churchill was elected prime minister
B. The Royal Air Force was formally established
C. Australia and New Zealand refused any further participation in the war
D. A major shakeup in the leadership of the Royal Navy ensued

17. What was the initial purpose of Britain's invasion of Mesopotamia?

    A. To open shipping routes on the Tigris and Euphrates rivers
    B. To liberate Kuwait
    C. To seize oil fields along the Persian Gulf
    D. To capture Tehran

18. Which best describes the outcome of Townshend's campaign in Mesopotamia?

    A. Ten thousand British troops were surrendered after a failed march on Baghdad
    B. Townshend's army took 100,000 Turkish prisoners of war in a single day
    C. The Ottoman Empire lost control of the entire region
    D. Constantinople was cut off from the Turkish mainland

19. How is the western front in World War I best characterized?

    A. A stagnant war fought from trenches, with neither side gaining or losing much ground in spite of huge casualties
    B. One of the most dynamic front lines of the twentieth century
    C. The first war front in history dominated by air power
    D. A mostly inactive front, along which both sides took a primarily defensive stance, resulting in relatively few casualties

20. Italy's action in the war was primarily against

    A. Germany
    B. Greece
    C. Austria-Hungary
    D. France

21. A war of attrition is defined as

A. A war in which both sides periodically exchange prisoners and then continue fighting
B. A war that is ended by a single crushing strike
C. A war that is won by cutting off the enemy's supply line
D. A war in which victory is determined not by which side seizes the most territory but by which side loses the most men

22. Which battle lasted for ten months, the longest of the war?

A. Battle of the Somme
B. Battle of Messines Ridge
C. Battle of Verdun
D. Battle of Passchendaele

23. Which country joined the war on the side of the Allied Powers in 1916?

A. Bulgaria
B. Greece
C. Serbia
D. Romania

24. What major change in German policy contributed to the United States entering the war?

A. An end to diplomatic relations with the United States
B. The declaration of unrestricted submarine warfare
C. Economic sanctions against the United States
D. An anti-British propaganda campaign in the American media, paid for by the German embassy

25. The Zimmermann telegram urged which country to attack the United States?

A. Mexico
B. Cuba
C. Panama
D. Canada

26. What country first intercepted the Zimmermann telegram?

    A. The United States
    B. Canada
    C. France
    D. Great Britain

27. What was the name of the first U.S. civilian ship to be sunk by a German submarine?

    A. *Lusitania*
    B. *Housatonic*
    C. *Titanic*
    D. *Maine*

28. On what date did the United States declare war on Germany?

    A. December 7, 1914
    B. April 6, 1917
    C. January 29, 1918
    D. November 4, 1917

29. Who was the commander of U.S. forces in Europe?

    A. Eddie Rickenbacker
    B. Dwight D. Eisenhower
    C. Theodore Roosevelt
    D. John J. Pershing

30. Following the declaration of war, U.S. forces

    A. Immediately attacked Germany
    B. Mobilized and deployed to Europe but did not enter combat for many months
    C. Concentrated on defending the U.S. mainland
    D. Went on alert but did not mobilize

31. What did Germany do in 1917 to hasten Russia's exit from the war?

- A. Hired mercenaries to assassinate the tsar
- B. Bombed food warehouses in major Russian cities
- C. Helped Russian revolutionaries in exile to get back to Russia
- D. Revealed that the tsar's German-born wife was spying for the kaiser

32. Which of the following best describes Lenin's role in the February Revolution?

- A. He was not involved
- B. As a member of the Duma, he put pressure on the tsar to abdicate
- C. He supplied arms to the demonstrators
- D. He planned the revolt

33. Who ordered the Russian offensive on July 1, 1917?

- A. Tsar Nicholas II
- B. Vladimir Lenin
- C. Alexander Kerensky
- D. Leon Trotsky

34. What was Lenin's first decree after the Bolshevik Revolution?

- A. An order that the Russian army surrender to Germany
- B. A request to the Central Powers to begin armistice negotiations
- C. A proclamation that Germany must be defeated at all costs
- D. A declaration of peace

35. Which best describes the outcome of Russia's peace negotiations?

- A. Russia gained territory
- B. Russia lost territory
- C. Russia neither gained nor lost territory
- D. Russian soldiers would have to serve in the German army on the western front

36. How did Russia's withdrawal affect the Allied forces?

    A. Allied troops were soon to be outnumbered by the Germans
    B. With Russia out of the picture, peace negotiations would become easier
    C. Without Russian help, Serbia fell to Austria-Hungary
    D. France withdrew from Alsace-Lorraine

37. In 1918, the city of Paris suffered repeated attacks from German

    A. Tanks
    B. Bombers
    C. Long-range artillery
    D. Poison gas shells

38. After declaring war, the United States was

    A. Officially part of the Central Powers
    B. At war only with Germany, not with Austria-Hungary
    C. Officially part of the Allied forces
    D. At war only with Austria-Hungary, not with Germany

39. Which of the following was a point of contention between the United States and the French and British?

    A. U.S. commanders refused to allow American troops to serve in French or British regiments
    B. The U.S. did not send any troops to Europe
    C. There were many unpleasant incidents between U.S. soldiers and local civilians
    D. U.S. commanders refused to coordinate their actions with Allied commanders

40. What pandemic disease threatened soldiers and civilians on all sides during the late stages of the war?

    A. Dysentery
    B. Measles
    C. Influenza
    D. Cholera

41. Which battle was the first major victory for American troops?

A. Cantigny
B. Lys
C. Moreuil Wood
D. Passchendaele

42. What country was the first of the Central Powers to surrender?

A. Italy
B. Austria-Hungary
C. Greece
D. Bulgaria

43. Who assumed power in Germany and led negotiations with the Allies after Wilhelm II lost power?

A. Max von Baden
B. Paul von Hindenburg
C. Otto von Bismarck
D. Manfred von Richthofen

44. Over which border region did fighting break out between Poland and Ukraine at the end of the war?

A. Sudetenland
B. East Galicia
C. Transylvania
D. Belorussia

45. Which new country was created as a "south Slavic state"?

A. Czechoslovakia
B. Bosnia-Herzegovina
C. Montenegro
D. Yugoslavia

46. What immediate condition was required of the Ottoman Empire in order to make peace?

    A. Constantinople had to be given back to Greece
    B. All troops had to be withdrawn from Gallipoli
    C. Free shipping had be reopened through the Dardanelles
    D. The ships *Goeben* and *Breslau* had to be returned to Germany

47. Where was the initial armistice with Germany negotiated?

    A. In the Reichstag building in Berlin
    B. In a train car near Compiègne, France
    C. At the Vatican
    D. At Versailles, France

48. Austria-Hungary made its armistice

    A. Jointly with Germany
    B. After negotiations with Russia held in Yalta
    C. After negotiations held in Italy
    D. At a formal ceremony at the White House

49. Which is true of Kaiser Wilhelm II?

    A. He abdicated voluntarily following a mutiny in the German navy
    B. Prince Max von Baden announced the kaiser's abdication without his consent
    C. He committed suicide
    D. He personally signed the armistice agreement

50. The formal peace treaty with Germany

A. Was signed under the Arc de Triomphe in Paris
B. Was signed on a ship sailing in neutral waters
C. Stipulated that Germany must give up its entire northern coastline
D. Was signed at Versailles

ANSWER KEY

1. D; 2. B; 3. A; 4. C; 5. C; 6. B; 7. A; 8. D; 9. B; 10. A; 11. B; 12. D; 13. A; 14. C; 15. A; 16. D; 17. C; 18. A; 19. A; 20. C; 21. D; 22. C; 23. D; 24. B; 25. A; 26. D; 27. B; 28. B; 29. D; 30. B; 31. C; 32. A; 33. C; 34. D; 35. B; 36. A; 37. C; 38. B; 39. A; 40. C; 41. A; 42. D; 43. A; 44. B; 45. D; 46. C; 47. B; 48. C; 49. B; 50. D

REVIEW & RESOURCES

Suggestions for Further Reading

FROMKIN, DAVID. *Europe's Last Summer: Who Started the Great War in 1914*. New York: Knopf, 2004.

FUSSELL, PAUL. *The Great War and Modern Memory*. New York: Oxford University Press, 1975.

GILBERT, MARTIN. *The First World War: A Complete History*. New York: Henry Holt, 1994.

HOWARD, MICHAEL. *The First World War*. Oxford: Oxford University Press, 2002.

MASSIE, ROBERT K. *Castles of Steel: Britain, Germany, and the Winning of the Great War at Sea*. New York: Random House, 2003.

STOKESBURY, JAMES L. *A Short History of World War I*. New York: William Morrow, 1981.